TANTRA YOGA,
NADA YOGA
AND KRIYA YOGA

TANTRA YOGA, NADA YOGA AND KRIYA YOGA

SRI SWAMI SIVANANDA

Published By

THE DIVINE LIFE SOCIETY

P.O. SHIVANANDANAGAR—249 192

Distt. Tehri-Garhwal, Uttarakhand, Himalayas, India

Price]   2009   [95/-

Seventh Edition: 2009

[1,000 Copies]

ISBN 81-7052-042-8

Published by Swami Vimalananda for The Divine
Life Society, Shivanandanagar, and printed by him
at the Yoga-Vedanta Forest Academy Press,
P.O. Shivanandanagar, Distt. Tehri-Garhwal,
Uttarakhand, Himalayas, India

TO

THE SUPREME DIVINE MOTHER

FULL OF LOVE AND COMPASSION

THE BESTOWER OF AUSPICIOUSNESS ON ALL

THIS WORK IS HUMBLY

DEDICATED

SRI SWAMI SIVANANDA

Born on the 8th September, 1887, in the illustrious family of Sage Appayya Dikshitar and several other renowned saints and savants, Sri Swami Sivananda had a natural flair for a life devoted to the study and practice of Vedanta. Added to this was an inborn eagerness to serve all and an innate feeling of unity with all mankind.

His passion for service drew him to the medical career; and soon he gravitated to where he thought that his service was most needed. Malaya claimed him. He had earlier been editing a health journal and wrote extensively on health problems. He discovered that people needed right knowledge most of all; dissemination of that knowledge he espoused as his own mission.

It was divine dispensation and the blessing of God upon mankind that the doctor of body and mind renounced his career and took to a life of renunciation to qualify for ministering to the soul of man. He settled down at Rishikesh in 1924, practised intense austerities and shone as a great Yogi, saint, sage and Jivanmukta.

In 1932 Swami Sivananda started the Sivanandashram. In 1936 was born The Divine Life Society. In 1948 the Yoga-Vedanta Forest Academy was organised. Dissemination of spiritual knowledge and training of people in Yoga and Vedanta were their aim and object. In 1950 Swamiji undertook a lightning tour of India and Ceylon. In 1953 Swamiji convened a 'World Parliament of Religions'. Swamiji is the author of over 300 volumes and has disciples all over the world, belonging to all nationalities, religions and creeds. To read Swamiji's works is to drink at the Fountain of Wisdom Supreme. On 14th July, 1963 Swamiji entered Mahasamadhi.

INTRODUCTION

The system called Tantra has been always regarded as an esoteric and a secret way of spiritual practice, not accessible to the untrained one and to the common folk. The secrecy about the practice seems to consist in the noble outlook of life which the Tantra requires the seeker to entertain, a way of looking at things different from the one in which people are generally accustomed to see, interpret and evaluate things. The teachers of the Tantra hold that a seeker on this path has to outgrow the social and even the human outlook and develop a superhuman and divine outlook in respect of things. Since this would be to expect too much from the common man in the world, Tantra is supposed to be a closed secret whose gates can be opened only with the key provided by a competent Guru.

The philosophy of the Tantra is based on the concept of a dual nature of everything. Nothing is single, but everything is bi-polar. The so-called unity of things is only a form taken by a particular manner of the coming together of two forces, Siva and Sakti, we may say, the positive and the negative poles. In order to understand this mystical conception of the universe, we may refer to the traditional doctrine of the Puranas, the Manusmriti and the Mahabharata, that in the beginning there was a universal Uni-Cell, as it were, known as the Brahmanda, which split into two, one part of which was the Cosmic

Man and another part the Cosmic Woman. We may call these parts Siva and Sakti, if we so wish. Even our modern science seems to be corroborating this view when it holds that in the beginning the universe was a single Atom, which split into two and then into the multiplicity of the present form of the universe. Since the two parts and their subsequent sub-divisions actually belong to a whole, there is a natural pull exerted by each on the other, there is a mutual attraction between the positive and the negative poles, both at the cosmic level and its lower multiple forms of descent, even down to the atom, which today we learn is constituted of a bi-polar structure with a nucleus in the centre and electrons revolving round it in a most mysterious way. The behaviour of the two parts of any single organism seems to be a double attitude of the consciousness of duality and unity at the same time. There cannot be attraction between the positive and the negative unless they form two poles, and not a single something, and yet, at the same time, there cannot be this attraction if they are absolutely two different things without a basic unity operating in and between them. This is the mystery and the difficulty in understanding the phenomenon known as attraction, usually called love or affection in common language.

While the concept of Siva and Sakti, in its highest essence, represents the Supreme Cosmic Duality, and one can imagine only attraction and love operating there, so that Siva and Sakti are considered as inseparable facets of a unitary reality sometimes known as Ardhanareesvara, the Cosmic Androgyne, the principle of repulsion, viz., dislike going with like, hatred going with love, will be seen at the lower levels where the bi-polar unity assumes a multiplicity of forms, so that one bi-polar unit cannot tolerate the interference or sometimes even the presence of another such bi-polar unit, for fear of losing its isolated self-conscious bi-polar unity. This subtle operation can be seen manifest in its grosser forms when one family group finds it difficult to appreciate another family group and bestow equal love upon it, one organisation, one social group, and even one bi-polar individual, cannot look upon another such without some suspicion and reservation.

According to the doctrine of the Tantra, the sorrow of life is caused by a bi-polar existence, a split of the one into two, because the truth of things is oneness and not the dual existence in any of its forms. The dual form of life being, in a sense, an unnatural way of life, there is always an ambivalent attitude of like and dislike at the same time between one pole and another, love getting suppressed when hate supervenes, and hate being suppressed when love gains the upper hand, while the fact is that both these attitudes are present in an individual hiddenly and only one of the aspects comes to the surface as and when the occasion demands. To get back from duality to unity is the process of Tantra Sadhana. While this is the objective of every Sadhana, what is the speciality of the Tantra as distinct from other Sadhana in the achievement of this objective?

The distinction is very subtle, not easily noticed. In all forms of religious practice, mostly, there is an ascetic injunction towards a rejection of the outer for the sake of the inner, the material for the sake of the spiritual, a cutting off of every desire as a baneful obstacle to Sadhana, and a considering of every joy in life as an evil to be eradicated at the earliest opportunity. To the Tantra, the things of the world, the material forms of perception, are not really obstacles, and a desire for them cannot be overcome by rejecting the desire itself. Everything in the world, the whole world itself, is a passage to perfection. The visible is a way to the invisible and not an obstacle to it. Human desires arise on account of the unintelligent attitude man develops towards desire, and he has a fear of desire since he is being told that all desires are bad and all objects are bondages. The Tantra holds that the object is not a bondage, because of the fact that the object is inseparably related to the subject, the object is the other pole of which the subject is the complementary pole. Every experience is a subject-object relation, and, therefore, no one can even think of overcoming the consciousness of the object, except by a relationship already established with the object. Thus, the attempt at overcoming the object involves one in a vicious circle. No effort in the direction of a getting rid of the object is possible, inasmuch as there is already a consciousness of the presence of the object. Thus, comes in the great dictum of the Tantra, that *desire can be overcome only by desire,* even as the object can be overcome only by the object. The other aspect of this principle held by the Tantra is that *"that by which one falls is also that by which one rises."* (Yaireva patanam dravyaih siddhih taireva).

Here is the crux of the whole matter regarding the Tantra, which marks it off from other religious practices and forms of Sadhana. Why this practice is difficult and even dangerous, will be obvious from the nature of the doctrine, while conceding that the doctrine is perhaps highly rational and based on a deep psychology of human nature.

The teachers of the Tantra know that there is a great difficulty in inculcating this doctrine and practising it. Hence, the art of Sadhana along this path is considered to be a graduated movement through different ascending stages of understanding and a disentanglement of the subject from involvement of the object, by a rising to a condition transcending the very relation between the subject and the object. The stages prescribed are, the Vedachara, the Vaishnavachara, Saivachara, Dakshinachara, Vamachara, Siddhantachara and, lastly, Kaulachara. Of these seven stages mentioned, the first three are intended for the lower category of Sadhakas, known as Pasujiva (persons in whom the animal nature is predominant), the next two for the Virajiva (persons in whom the normal human instinct is predominant), and the last two for the Divyajiva (person in whom the divine element is predominant). It is believed that the first three Acharas stand, respectively, for Karma. Bhakti and Jnana, the Veda standing for ritual, Vaishnava for devotion and Saiva standing for knowledge. The fourth Achara, which is called Dakshina, attempts to conserve the results achieved through the practice of the first three stages. Up to this level, the movement is almost linear and a straight one, practically. But at the next stage of Vamachara, there is a strange difference in outlook, for this term implies the commencement of the return current of the soul's movement towards reality. 'Vama' does not mean 'left', as most people seem to think, but the 'reverse' process, *Nivritti* or returning, as distinguished from *Pravritti* or flowing onward along the natural current of the senses. Here is the beginning of the most secret practice or the esoteric aspect of the Tantra Sadhana, where objects of attraction, whatever be their nature, are regarded as instruments, not to be rejected, but assimilated into and made part and parcel of one's own being, but with the intention of overcoming the consciousness that they are outside oneself as a sort of opposing object or an external something. This particular phase is not supposed to be explained, but learnt directly from a Master. The greatest obstacles to spiritual perfection are generally considered to be wealth, power and sex, and it is these that the Tantra intends to harness and overcome by the very means by which an untrained mind may head towards a fall. The Pasu, Vira and Divya Bhavas, corresponding to the animal, human and divine natures, take into consideration the gross, the subtle and the divine aspects of the things which are to be confronted as oppositions in one's spiritual life. This is the forbidden area of Tantra Sadhana, which no true seeker will disclose, as the common man is not expected to know it, understand it, or be benefited by it. Every object has a gross form, a subtle form, and a divine form, and every Sadhaka has to pass through all these stages. The Tantra insists that no stage can be rejected as an obstacle but has to be traversed personally. An unknown thing, an object of fear, cannot come under one's control.

The Trantra holds that the impure, the ugly and the unholy things of life are things which have been wrongly seen out of their context, and, from their own particular positions, or from the point of view of the things themselves, they are neither good nor bad, neither beautiful nor ugly, neither holy nor unholy. These are all suggestions given by the mind from the standpoint of the particular interest which refuses to take into consideration that there can be other interests than one's own. The universe is a multi-point of view, and not a single point of view; from the former one has to rise to the latter, by a systematic and progressive movement of the whole of one's being through the gross, the subtle and the divine compositions of things. In the beginning, one contacts the object. Next, one merely thinks it in the mind. Lastly, one visualises it as a point of stress in the Universal Reality. The Siddhantachara and the Kaulachara mentioned above complete the process of Sadhana, whereby one gets established in the true nature of things and becomes veritably superhuman. The renunciation involved in religious practice is not a rejection of the object or the thing as such, but the idea or the notion that it is outside oneself. It is this wrong idea that generates desire, not the object or the thing. The prescription is indeed very subtle.

Tantra Sadhana includes the recitation of Mantras, performance of rituals through Yantras and an adjustment of oneself to the particular degree of reality, which is the specific meaning of Tantra. In this process, one has to learn many minor details directly from the Guru. The purification of the body, the mind and one's social relations, are all important preparations of the Sadhana. The usual Shodasopachara-Puja or the sixteen-limbed worship addressed to a Deity, is also the procedure applicable to anything and everything that one adores, regards or loves. By worship, one seeks union with the Deity through an abolition of the separation of oneself from the Deity. The mysterious processes called Nyasa (Anga-Nyasa and Kara-Nyasa) are, again, inward techniques of feeling the object in oneself, the Deity in one's own being. All this would make it abundantly clear that the Tantra Sadhana is as highly scientific and precise, as it is difficult and dangerous. This is its speciality.

Swami Krishnananda

CONTENTS

BOOK TWO

NADA YOGA

BOOK THREE

KRIYA YOGA

TANTRA YOGA, NADA YOGA AND KRIYA YOGA

BOOK ONE

TANTRA YOGA

TANTRA YOGA

Salutations to the Mother who is the Parabrahman of the Vedantins, the Parama-Siva of Saiva Siddhantins, the Maha-Vishnu of the Vaishnavites; who is the Father in Heaven of the Christians, Allah of the Mohammedans, Jehovah of the Jews, Nirvana of Bauddhas, Ahura Mazda of Zoroastrians, the Thing-in-itself of occidental philosophers, the God Almighty of all religions.

The Sakti philosophy is as old as the Vedas. The Devi Sukta in the Rig Veda is the real source of the Sakti doctrine. The Devi is not only the principle of creation, the principle of auspiciousness, the principle of cosmic energy, but is also the principle of Divine Knowledge. The glory of the Devi is most elaborately sung in the Sakta Agamas and Tantras and in the Devi Bhagavata also.

Maha Devi or Mahesvari or Parasakti is the Supreme Sakti or Power of the Supreme Being. She is the Creatrix of the universe. Durga, Tripurasundari, Lalita, Raja Rajesvari are all forms of Para Sakti or Mula Prakriti or Chit Sakti or Brahma Sakti.

In the Sakti doctrine Siva is the supreme unchanging eternal consciousness and Sakti is His kinetic power. Universe is Power. Universe is a manifestation of Devi's glory. This is the affirmation of the Sakti doctrine. Sakti being the Power of God, Sakta is one who possesses Sakti.

Tantra Sadhana bestows tremendous Siddhis or powers. It should be learnt under a Siddha Tantric Guru. The Tantric student must be endowed with purity, faith, devotion, dedication to Guru, dispassion, humility, courage, cosmic love, truthfulness, non-covetousness and contentment. Absence of these qualities in the practitioner means a gross abuse of Saktism.

Saktism had been one of the potent powers for the spiritual regeneration of the Hindus. When practised by the ignorant, unenlightened and unqualified persons, it has led to certain abuses; and there is no denying that some degraded forms of Saktism have sought nothing but magic, immorality, and occult powers. An example of the perverted expression of the truth, a travesty of the original practices, is the theory of the five *Makaras*—*madya* or wine, *mamsa* or flesh, *matsya* or fish, *mudra* or symbolical acts and *maithuna* or coitus.

The Sakti Tantra is Advaita Vada. It proclaims that Paramatma and Jivatma are one. The Saktas accept the Vedas as the basic scriptures. They recognise the Sakta-Tantras as texts expounding the means to attain the goal set forth in the Vedas.

Tantra system is an integral part of Hinduism. Sakti system is one of the most important of Eastern systems. Tantra Sastra deserves a careful and deep study. The fundamental ideas of this system are in accordance with reason. The teachings of the Tantras are very correct. The Sakta Tantra is a Sadhana Sastra of Advaita Vedanta. It is indeed a deep and powerful system.

Mahanirvana, Kularnava Tantra are the important books in Tantra Sastra. Yoga Kundalini Upanishad of Krishna Yajurveda, Yoga Tattva Upanishad of Krishna Yajurveda, Jabala Darsana, Trishikh Brahmana, Varaha Upanishad are useful for getting knowledge of Kundalini Sakti and the methods to awaken it and take it to Sahasrara Chakra at the crown of the head.

The Tantras are not books of sorcery or witchcraft, magic spells and mysterious formulae. They are wonderful scriptures. All persons without the distinctions of caste, creed, or colour may draw inspiration and attain spiritual strength, wisdom and eternal bliss. They are Sadhana Sastras. They show the path to liberation, perfection, freedom and immortal bliss.

Tantra is the saving wisdom. It is the marvellous boat which takes man safely to the other shore of fearlessness, immortality, freedom and perfection.

Tantra explains (Tanoti) in great detail the knowledge concerning Tattva (Truth or Brahman) and Mantra (mystic syllables). It saves (Tranat). Hence it is called Tantra.

The Tantra is in some of its aspects a secret doctrine. It is a Gupta Vidya. You cannot learn it from the study of books. You will have to get the knowledge and practice from the practical Tantriks, the Tantric Acharyas and Gurus who hold the key to it.

The word "Sakti" comes from the root "Sakt" which means "to be able," "to do." Sakti is symbolically female, but it is in reality neither male nor female, but only a force which manifests itself in various forms. Earth, water, fire, air, ether, electricity are Her gross forms—Apara Prakriti.

Life element is Her Para Prakriti. Mind is a modification of Chit Sakti.

Tantra Yoga lays special emphasis on the development of the powers latent in the six Chakras, from Muladhara to Ajna.

Sadhakas are of three kinds, viz., Pasu, Veera and Divya. It is only the Pasu Sadhakas who practise the Pancha Makaras, viz., Matsya, Mamsa, Madya, Mudra and Maithuna (coition). The esoteric meaning of these five Makaras is "kill egoism, control flesh, drink the wine of God-intoxication and have union with Lord Siva." This is the divine practice of Divya Sadhakas who lead the life divine. Give up Pasu Vritti, the tendency of animals and raise the Divya Vritti or the divine nature.

May Para-Sakti, or Devi—the Universal Mother Jagadamba bless you all with wisdom, peace and Immortal Bliss.

SAKTI YOGA PHILOSOPHY

I

The power or active aspect of the immanent God is Sakti. Sakti is the embodiment of power. She is the supporter of the vast universe. She is the supreme Power by which the world is upheld. She is the Universal Mother. She is Durga, Kali, Chandi, Chamundi, Tripurasundari, Rajarajesvari. There is no difference between God and His Sakti, just as there is no difference between fire and its burning power.

He who worships Sakti, that is God in Mother form, as the Supreme Power which creates, sustains and withdraws the universe, is a Sakta. All women are the forms of Divine Mother.

Siva is the unchanging consciousness. Sakti is His changing Power which appears as mind and matter. Sakti-vada or Sakta-darshana is a form of monism or Advaita-vada.

A Sakta does Sadhana which helps the union of Siva and Sakti through the awakening of the forces within the body. He becomes a Siddha in the Sadhana when he is able to awaken Kundalini and pierce the six Chakras. This is to be done in a perfectly practical way under the guidance of a Guru who has become perfect. The Sakti must be awakened by Dhyana, Bhava, Japa and Mantra Sakti. The Mother, the embodiment of the fifty letters is present in the various letters in the different Chakras. When the chords of a musical instrument are struck harmoniously, fine music is produced. Even so, when the chords of the letters are struck in their order, the Mother who moves in the six Chakras and who is the very Self of the letters awakens Herself. The Sadhaka attains Siddhi easily when She is roused. It is difficult to say when and how She shows Herself and to what Sadhaka. Sadhana means unfolding, rousing up or awakening of power of Sakti. Mode of Sadhana depends upon the tendencies and capacities of the Sadhaka.

Sakti may be termed as that by which we live and have our being in this universe. In this world all the wants of the child are provided by the Mother. The child's growth, development and sustenance are looked after by the Mother. Even so all the necessaries of life and its activities in this world and the energy needed for it depend upon Sakti or the universal Mother.

No one can free himself from the thraldom of mind and matter without Mother's grace. The fetters of Maya are too hard to break. If you worship Her as the great Mother you can very easily go beyond Prakriti through Her benign grace and blessings. She will remove all obstacles in the path and lead you safely into the illimitable domain of eternal Bliss and make you absolutely free. When She is pleased and bestows Her blessings on you, then alone can you free yourself from the bondage of this formidable Samsara.

The first syllable which a child or a quadruped utters is the name of the beloved Mother. Is there any child who does not owe its all to the affection and love of its Mother? It is the Mother who protects you, consoles you, cheers you and nurses you. She is your friend, philosopher, preceptor and guide throughout your life. Human mother is a manifestation of the Universal Mother.

The supreme Lord is represented as Siva and His power is represented as His wife, Sakti, Durga, or Kali. Just as the husband and wife look after the well-being of the family, so also Lord Siva and His Sakti are engaged in looking after the affairs of this world.

Radha, Durga, Lakshmi, Sarasvati and Savitri are the five primary forms of Prakriti or Devi. Durga destroyed Madhu and Kaitabha through Vishnu. As Mahalakshmi She destroyed the Asura Mahisha. And as Sarasvati She destroyed Sumbha and Nisumbha with their companions Dhumralochana, Chanda, Munda and Raktabija.

When Vishnu and Mahadeva destroyed various Asuras, the Power of Devi was behind them. Devi took Brahma, Vishnu and Rudra and gave them necessary Sakti to proceed with the work of creation, preservation and destruction. She is at the centre of the life of the universe. She is in the Muladhara Chakra in our bodies. She vitalises the body through the Sushumna. She vitalises the universe from the summit of Mount Meru.

In this system of Sakti philosophy Siva is omnipresent, impersonal, inactive. He is pure consciousness. Sakti is dynamic. Siva and Sakti are related as Prakasa and Vimarsa. Sakti or Vimarsa is the power that is latent in the pure consciousness. Vimarsa gives rise to the world of distinctions. Siva is Chit. Sakti is Chidrupini. Brahma, Vishnu and Siva do their functions of creation, preservation and destruction in obedience to Sakti. Sakti is endowed with Iccha (will), Jnana (knowledge) and Kriya (action). Siva and Sakti are one. Sakti Tattva and Siva Tattva are inseparable. Siva is always with Sakti.

There are thirty-six Tattvas in Sakti philosophy. Sakti is in Sakti Tattva, Nada is in Sadakhya Tattva, and Bindu is in Isvara Tattva. The creative aspect of the supreme Siva is called Siva Tattva. Siva Tattva is the first creative movement. Sakti Tattva is the will of Siva. It is the seed and womb of the entire world.

The first manifestation is called the Sadakhya or Sadasiva Tattva. In this Tattva there is the beginning of formation of ideas. There is Nada Sakti in this Tattva. Next comes Isvara Tattva. This Tattva is called Bindu. The fourth Tattva is Vidya or Suddhavidya. Then Prakriti modifies into the Tattvas of the mind, senses and the matter which constitutes the world.

Nada, Bindu are all names for different aspects of Sakti, Nada is really Siva Sakti. Siva has two aspects. In one aspect, He is the supreme changeless One, who is

Sat-Chit-Ananda. This is Para Samvit. In the other aspect He changes as the world. The cause of the change is Siva Tattva. This Siva Tattva and Sakti Tattva are inseparable. Sakti Tattva is the first dynamic aspect of Brahman.

Nishkala Siva is Nirguna Siva. He is not connected with the creative Sakti. Maya or Prakriti is within the womb of the Sakti. Maya is the matrix of the world. Maya is potential in the state of dissolution. She is dynamic in creation. Maya evolved into several material elements and other physical parts of all sentient creatures under the direction of Sakti. There are thirty-six Tattvas in Sakti philosophy. In Sakti philosophy we have Brahman, Nada, Sakti, Bindu and Suddhamaya. In Saiva Siddhanta philosophy we have Siva, Sakti, Sadakhya and the Suddhamaya. The rest of the evolution in Sakti philosophy is same as in Saiva Siddhanta philosophy.

Knowledge of the Sakti leads to salvation. "*Sakti-Jnanam vina Devi nirvanam naiva jayate*"—"O Devi without the knowledge of Sakti, Mukti cannot be attained" (Isvara says to Devi). The Jiva or the individual soul thinks, when he is under the influence of Maya, that he is the doer and the enjoyer and identifies himself with the body. Through the grace of Sakti and through Sadhana or self-culture the individual soul frees himself from all fetters and attains spiritual insight and merges himself in the Supreme.

There is in Reality nothing but the one Self. The experienced is nothing but the experiencer. Brahman appears as the world through the mirror of mind or Maya. An object is nothing but the one Self appearing through Maya as non-self to Itself as subject. Triputi (or the knower, knowledge, knowable) vanishes in Nirvikalpa Samadhi. Supreme Siva or Brahman alone exists.

In the Kenopanishad it is said that the gods became puffed up with pride after a victory over the Asuras. They wrongly took the success to be the result of their own valour and power. The Lord wanted to teach them a lesson. He appeared before them in the form of a Yaksha, a huge form, the beginning and end of which were not visible. The Devas wanted to find out the identity of this form and sent Agni for this purpose. The Yaksha asked Agni, "What is thy name and power?" Agni replied, "I am Agni (Jatavedas). I can burn up the whole universe in a minute." The Yaksha placed before Agni a dry blade of grass and asked him to burn it. Agni was not able to burn it. He ran away from the Yaksha in shame. The gods sent Vayu to enquire who he was. Vayu approached the Yaksha. The Yaksha asked Vayu, "Who are you? What is your power?" Vayu replied, " I am wind-god. I can blow the whole world in a minute." The Yaksha then placed a blade of grass before Vayu and challenged him to blow it away. Vayu could not make it move an inch from its place. He too left the place in shame. Last of all came Indra himself. When Indra reached the place, he found that the Yaksha had vanished. Then Uma appeared before Indra and revealed to him the real identity of the Yaksha. She said to Indra: "It is the power of the Divine Mother and not that of the gods that crowned the gods with victory. It is Sakti of Uma or Haimavati, sister of Krishna that is the source of the strength of all the gods." Sakti is the great Teacher of Jnana. She sheds wisdom on Her devotees.

II

Sakti is Chidroopini. She is pure, blissful pure Consciousness. She is the Mother of Nature. She is Nature Itself. She is the Power of Lord Siva or Brahman. She runs this world show. She maintains the sportive Lila of the Lord. She is Jagat-Janani, Creator of the world, Mahishasuramardini, destroyer of Mahishasura, Bhrantinasini (destroyer of the illusion or Avidya), and Daridranasini (destroyer of poverty).

Devi is Sakti of Lord Siva. She is Jada Sakti and Chit Sakti. Sakti is Prakriti, Maya, Mahamaya, Sri Vidya. Sakti is Brahman itself. She is Lalita, Kundalini, Rajarajesvari and Tripurasundari, Sakti manifested to Lord Siva in the ten forms as the Dasa Maha Vidya, viz., Kali, Bagalamukhi, Chinnamastak, Bhuvanesvari, Matangi, Shodasi, Dhoomavati, Tripurasundari, Tara and Bhairavi.

Worship of Sakti or Saktism is one of the oldest and most widespread religions in the world. Everybody in this world wants power, loves to possess power. He is elated by power. He wants to domineer over others through power. War is the outcome of greed for power. Scientists are followers of Saktism. He who wishes to develop will-power and a charming personality is a follower of Saktism. In reality, every man in this world is a follower of Saktism.

Scientists say now that everything is energy only and that energy is the physical ultimate of all forms of matter. The followers of the Sakta school of philosophy have said the same thing long ago. They further say that this energy is only the limited manifestation of the Infinite Supreme Power or Maha Sakti.

Sakti is always with Siva. They are inseparable like fire and heat. Sakti evolves Nada and Nada Bindu. The world is manifestation of Sakti. Suddha Maya is Chit-Sakti. Prakriti is Jada Sakti. Nada, Bindu and the rest are only names for different aspects of Sakti.

The countless universes are only the dust of divine Mother's Holy feet. Her glory is ineffable. Her splendour is indescribable. Her greatness is unfathomable. She showers Her grace on Her sincere devotees. She leads the individual Soul from Chakra to Chakra, from plane to plane and unites him with Lord Siva in the Sahasrara.

The body is Sakti. The needs of the body are the needs of Sakti. When man enjoys, it is Sakti who enjoys through him. His eyes, ears, hands and feet are Hers. She sees through his eyes, works through his hands, and hears through his ears. Body, mind, Prana, egoism, intellect, organs and all the other functions are Her manifestations.

Saktism speaks of personal and the Impersonal aspects of Godhead. Brahman is Nishkala or without Prakriti and Sakala or with Prakriti. The Vedantins speak of Nirupadhika Brahman (pure Nirguna Brahman without Maya) and Sopadhika Brahman (Saguna Brahman with Upadhi or Maya). It is all the same. Names only are different. It is a play of words or Sabda-jalam. People fight on words only and carry on lingual warfare, hair-splitting, logical chopping and intellectual gymnastics. In reality the essence is One. Clay only is Truth; all modifications such as pot, etc., are in name only. In Nirguna Brahman, Sakti is potential whereas in Saguna Brahman Sakti is dynamic.

The basis of Saktism is the Veda. Saktism upholds that the only source and authority (Pramana) regarding transcendental or supersensual matters such as the nature of Brahman, etc., is Veda. Saktism is only Vedanta.The Saktas have the same spiritual experience as that of a Vedantin.

The Devi-Sookta of the Rig-Veda, the Sri-Sookta, Durga-Sookta, Bhoo-Sookta and Neela-Sookta and the specific Sakta Upanishads such as Tripurasundari Upanishad, Sitopanishad, Devi Upanishad, Saubhyaga Upanishad, Sarasvati Upanishad, Bhavanopanishad, Bahvrichopanishad, etc., all emphatically delcare the Mother aspect of God. The Kena Upanishad also speaks of Uma, Haimavati who imparted wisdom of the Self to Indra and the Devas.

Divine Mother is everywhere triple. She is endowed with the three Gunas, *viz.,* Sattva, Rajas, Tamas. She manifests as Will (Iccha Sakti), Action (Kriya Sakti) and Knowledge (Jnana Sakti). She is Brahma Sakti (Sarasvati) in conjunction with Brahma, Vishnu Sakti (Lakshmi) in conjunction with Lord Vishnu, Siva Sakti (Gouri) in conjunction with Lord Siva. Hence She is called Tripurasundari.

The abode of Tripurasundari, the Divine Mother, is called Sri-Nagara; this magnificent abode is surrounded by twenty-five ramparts which represent the twenty-five Tattvas. The resplendent Chintamani Palace is in the middle. The Divine Mother sits in the Bindu Peetha in Sri Chakra in that wonderful palace. There is a similar abode for Her in the body of man also. The whole world is Her body. Mountains are Her bones. Rivers are Her veins. Ocean is Her bladder. Sun, moon are Her eyes. Wind is her breath. Agni is Her mouth.

The Sakta enjoys Bhukti (enjoyment in the world) and Mukti (liberation from all worlds.) Siva is an embodiment of Bliss and Knowledge. Siva Himself appears in the form of man with a life of pleasure and pain. If you remember this point always, dualism, all hatred, jealousy and pride will vanish. You must consider every human function as worship or a religious act. Answering calls of nature, micturition, talking, eating, walking, seeing, hearing—all become worship of Lord, if you develop the right attitude. It is Siva who works in and through man. Where then is egoism and individuality? All human actions are divine actions. One universal life throbs in the heart of all, sees in the eyes of all, works in the hands of all and hears in the ears of all. What a magnanimous experience it is, if one can feel this by crushing this little 'I'! The old Samskaras, the old Vasanas, the old habits of thinking stand in the way of your realising this Experience-whole.

The aspirant thinks that the world is identical with the divine Mother. He moves about thinking his own form to be the form of the divine Mother and thus beholds oneness everywhere. He also feels that the Divine Mother is identical with Brahman.

The advanced Sadhaka feels: "I am the Devi and the Devi is me." He worships himself as Devi instead of adoring any external object. He says "Soham" "I am She (Devi)."

Saktism is not mere theory or philosophy. It prescribes systematic Sadhana of Yoga, regular discipline according to the temperament, capacity and degree of evolution of the Sadhaka. It helps the aspirant to arouse the Kundalini and unite Her with Lord Siva, and to enjoy the supreme bliss or Nirvikalpa Samadhi. When

Kundalini sleeps, man is awake to the world. He has objective consciousness. When She awakes, he sleeps. He loses all consciousness of the world and becomes one with the Lord. In Samadhi the body is maintained by the nectar which flows from the union of Siva and Sakti in Sahasrara.

Guru is indispensable for the practice of Sakti Yoga Sadhana. He initiates the aspirant and transmits the divine Sakti.

Physical contact with a female is gross Maithuna. This is due to Pasu-bhava or animal attraction or brutal instinct. Mother Kundalini Sakti unites with Lord Siva in Sahasrara during Nirvikalpa Samadhi. This is real Maithuna or blissful union. This is due to Divya-bhava or divine disposition. You must rise from Pasu-bhava to Divya-bhava, through Satsanga, service of Guru, renunciation and dispassion, discrimination, Japa and meditation.

Worship of the Divine Mother, intense faith and perfect devotion and self-surrender will help you to attain Her grace. Through Her grace alone, can you attain knowledge of the Imperishable.

Glory to Sri Tripurasundari, the world Mother, who is also Rajarajesvari and Lalita Devi. May their blessings be upon you all!

MOTHER WORSHIP

Mother worship is the worship of God as Divine Mother-Sri Mata. Sakti is the power of the Lord or the cosmic energy. Sakti is the energy aspect of Isvara or the Lord. Sakti is inherent in God. Just as you cannot separate heat from fire, so also you cannot separate Sakti from God, the Sakta or the possessor of Sakti. Sakti and Sakta are one. They are inseparable. Worship of Durga or Parvati or Kali is worship of Lord Siva. The Divine Mother, in Her aspect of Durga, is represented as having ten different weapons in Her ten hands, and as sitting on a lion.

Electricity, magnetism, force, heat, light, the five elements and their combinations are all eternal manifestations of Sakti. Intelligence, discrimination, psychic power and will are all Her internal manifestations. She keeps up the Lila of the Lord through the three Gunas—Sattva, Rajas, and Tamas—Vidya, Shanti, lust, anger, greed, egoism and pride are all Her forms. Her manifestations are countless. Durga, Kali, Bhagavati, Bhavani, Ambal, Ambika, Jagadamba, Kamesvari, Ganga, Uma, Chandi, Chamundi, Lalita, Gouri, Kundalini, Tara, Rajarajesvari, Tripurasundari, etc., are all Her forms. She is Para Sakti, Radha, Durga, Lakshmi, Sarasvati and Savitri, are the five Prakritis. She is worshipped during the nine days of the Dussara as Durga, Lakshmi and Sarasvati.

She lies dormant in the Muladhara Chakra in the form of serpentine power or coiled up energy known as the "Kundalini Sakti." She is at the centre of the life of the universe. She is the primal force of life that underlies all existence. She vitalises the body through the Sushumnanadi and nerves. She nourishes the body with chyle and blood. She vitalises the universe through Her energy. She is the energy in the Sun, the fragrance in the flowers, the beauty in the landscape, the Gayatri or the Blessed Mother in the Vedas, colour in the rainbow, intelligence in the mind, potency in the homoeopathic pills, power in Makaradhvaja and gold oxide, will and Vichara Sakti in sages, devotion in Bhaktas, Samyama and Samadhi in Yogins.

You are more free with your mother than with anybody else. You open your heart more freely to your mother than to your father. *Na Matuh Paramadaivatam*—there is no God greater than the mother. It is the mother who protects you, nourishes you, consoles you, cheers you and nurses you. She is your first Guru. The first syllable which almost every quadruped or human being utters is the beloved name of the mother (Ma). She sacrifices her all for the sake of her children.

A child is more familiar with mother than with the father, because the former is very kind, loving, tender, affectionate and looks after the wants of the child. Whenever the child wants anything, it runs with outstretched hands to the mother, rather than to the father. If she hears the cry of the child, she leaves her domestic work and runs immediately to attend to the child. In the spiritual field also, the aspirant or the devotee—the spiritual child—has more intimate relationship with Mother Durga than with the Father Siva. Lord Siva is quite indifferent to the external world. He is a Tyagi and a Virakta, He wears the garlands of skulls of His devotees, rubs the whole body with Vibhuti or holy ash and remains in the crematorium in an intoxicated state. He is absorbed in contemplation of the Self. He remains in a state of Nirvikalpa Samadhi. He has handed over the power of attorney to His consort, Durga. It is Mother Durga only who looks after the affairs of the world. Lord Siva (Purusha) gazes at Prakriti (Durga), His Sakti. She engages Herself in creation, preservation and destruction.

It behoves, therefore, that the aspirant should approach the Mother first, so that She may introduce Her spiritual child to the Father for its illumination or Self-realisation. That is the reason why the devotees have placed Radha, Sita, Gouri, first in the Yugala-Namas, viz., Radha Krishna, Sita Rama, Gouri Sankar, Uma Sankar, Bhavani Sankar, Lakshmi Narayana.

The Upasana or worship of Devi or Universal Mother leads to the attainment of knowledge of the Self. The story in the Kenopanishad known as `Yaksha Prasna' supports this view, where Uma taught the Truth to the Devas.

Mother's grace is boundless. Her mercy is illimitable. Her knowledge is infinite. Her power is immeasurable. Her glory is ineffable. Her splendour is indescribable. She gives you Bhukti (material prosperity) and Mukti (liberation) also.

Approach Her with an open heart. Lay bare your heart before Her with frankness and humility. Be simple as a child. Kill ruthlessly egoism, cunningness, selfishness and crookedness. Make a total, unreserved, ungrudging surrender to Her. Sing Her prise. Repeat Her name. Worship Her with faith and unflinching devotion. Do special Puja on Navaratri days. Navaratri is the most suitable occasion for doing intense Sadhana. Those nine days are very sacred to Devi. Plunge yourself in Her worship. Do Anushthana. Devi fought with Bhandasura and his force for nine days and nine nights. The war ended on the evening of the tenth day known as `Vijaya Dasami' or the 'day of victory.' Akshara Abhyasa for children is done on the Vijaya Dasami day. Aspirants are initiated on this day. The beginning of learning of any science is done on this most auspicious day. It was on this day that Arjuna worshipped the Devi before starting the fight against the Kauravas in the field of Kurukshetra.

May the Divine Mother Durga establish righteousness or Dharma in the world! May She destroy all dark hostile forces that disturb the peace of the world! May She remove all sorts of epidemics and famines from the land! May She bring supreme peace, prosperity and undying bliss to all Her children of this world! May She transmute the Asuras or the demons or people with diabolical tendencies into Sattvic men! May She annihilate the Asuric tendencies, such as lust, anger, pride, hypocrisy, etc., in human beings, which represent, Madhu, Kaitabha, Mahisha, Sumbha and Nisumbha!

May She give the milk of divine wisdom to Her children and lift them up to the magnanimous heights of divine splendour and glory, the imperishable state of Kaivalya and eternal sunshine!

ANANDA LAHARI

"Saundarya Lahari" means "the wave of beauty" because it gives a description of the physical beauty or the bodily perfection of the Devi's form (Sthularupa). "Ananda Lahari" means "the wave of bliss." The first forty-one stanzas encompass the 'Ananda Lahari' and the other verses constitute `Saundarya Lahari.' The author of this wonderful book is Sri Sankarcharya, the great intellectual genius and Vedantic preacher of Southern India, who was born at Kaladi (Malabar). Among the hymns addressed to Devi, the 'Saundarya Lahari' occupies a unique position. It is one of the most inspiring of devotional poems.

'Ananda Lahari' deals with the Kundalini Yoga and the Chakras and other Tantrik subjects. It is a very important work on Tantra Sastra. It contains the essence of Sri Vidya in a nutshell. Hence, it has got the largest number of commentaries.

'Ananda Lahari' is a Tantrik text which deals with the worship of the Supreme Being in its (feminine) aspect of the Sakti or power or the creative energy known as Sri-Vidya. Practice of Sri-Vidya is adopted by many people in Southern India, particularly in Malabar.

'Ananda Lahari' contains beautiful poems which contain Sutras or hymns in praise of Devi or the goddess, Tripurasundari. The stanzas exhibit the highest flights of imagination, remarkable devotional fervour, exquisite touches of poetical fancy and an insight into the secrets of the Agamas and the Tantras. The stanzas contain various Mantras or mystical formula, along with Yantras or diagrams, for worship of Devi and for the attainment of various Siddhis or powers.

Worship of Devi in the form of Sri-Vidya is of two kinds, viz., internal, for advanced students, and external for the less evolved students. In the internal form of worship there are neither rituals nor ceremonies. The Supreme Being, in the aspect of Siva united with the Sakti, is worshipped at the various centres of energy of the human body or Chakras or lotuses. Those who perform the internal mode of worship believe in the identity of Siva and Sakti, in the awakening of Kundalini and in taking it up, through the various Chakras to Sahasrara or the thousand-petalled lotus, through worship, Japa of Mantra, where the individual soul unites with the Supreme Soul.

In the external form of worship Sri-Chakra is worshipped. Yantra is inscribed on gold or other metallic plates. Mantras are repeated with gestures, postures, waving of light or Arati and offerings of incense, Naivedya or various sorts of food or Prasad.

Each verse has a Yantra with Bija-Aksharas and a prescribed course of worship. The Bija-Aksharas and Yantra are inscribed on a gold or copper plate. The food offerings to the Devi vary according to the mode of worship and the purpose. There is a definite distinctive aim to be achieved by a particular mode of worship with a particular Yantra and a particular offering. The days of worship also vary from 4 to 180 days. Wealth, learning, lordship, success in enterprise, mastery over the elements, eloquence, poetic talents, conquest over the enemy, eradication of incurable ailments, etc., can be attained by worship of Devi, in different Yantras, with different Bija-Aksharas and different offerings. Worldly people generally use the verses of the hymn for invoking the Devi for the fulfilment of worldly desires. Success depends upon the faith and devotion of the aspirant. If there is any delay in the attainment of the specific fruit, you will have to worship for some more days with intense devotion. These verses can help you in the attainment of the final beautitude of life also, if you seek that alone from the Divine Mother.

Above Sakti and Siva, various manifestations of Para-Sakti and Sada-Siva exist. The body of Maha-Sakti or Para-Sakti is formed of pure and concentrated Sattva without any admixture of Rajas and Tamas. The other Saktis have merely a preponderance of the Sattva over

Rajas or Tamas and not of pure Sattva. Therefore, She is the highest, the prototype of Para-Brahman.

The different Saktis are: Para-Sakti, Adi-Sakti, Iccha-Sakti, Kriya-Sakti, Jnana-Sakti, Bala, Tripura-sundari, Rajarajesvari, Annapurna, Gayatri, Savitri, Kundalini and many others. Though each nature produces a specific result, yet it may also produce a general result. You may repeat any one of the names of the Devi. If you wish to obtain a particular fruit, you must invoke the goddess by the corresponding name.

Just as the fruit is hidden in the seed, butter in milk, virility in boyhood, so also various Saktis remain latent in man, veiled by ignorance. If you purify your mind and practise concentration and meditation, all these powers will shine forth.

The highest fruit of meditation or Upasana is the identity or non-distinction with the object meditated upon. The meditator and the meditated become one. The devotee of Devi attains realisation of oneness with Devi through intense Upasana or worship.

The Kurma Purana says: "Water is able to quench the fire, the presence of the sun to dispel darkness, and the repetition of the names of Devi to destroy the multitude of sins in the Kali age." The Brahma Purana says: "Those who worship the Supreme Sakti, whether regularly or irregularly, are not entangled in Samsara. There is no doubt they are the liberated souls."

A study of Ananda Lahari daily in the early morning will be a great help to all who desire material as well as spiritual progress. Get up early in the morning at 4 a.m. Have your bath and other purificatory acts. Then perform

----

your Nitya Karma in a separate Puja room. Place therein the photos of your Ishta Devata, your Guru and that of Tripurasundari, the World Mother and generatrix of this universe in whose praise Ananda Lahari is sung. After performing your Nitya Karma have a full reading of Ananda Lahari with extreme faith and devotion. Keep a ghee lamp burning throughout your Puja time. In the end, wave lights, burn incense and camphor before the Devi, your Ishta Devata and others. Place the offerings of coconut, honey, milk, fruits, etc., before the deity and take the sacred Prasad. If you are not able to read the whole 'Ananda Lahari' daily study at least five Slokas or even one Sloka with intense faith and devotion. Do this regularly without fail.

This will relieve you of all pains, miseries and tribulations. You will attain high position and success in life and ultimately attain Sayujya Mukti. Pray to Mother Goddess with a melting heart with faith and devotion. I assure you, you will have rapid success in life and spiritual progress.

CLASSIFICATION OF ASPIRANTS

Pasu, Vira, Divya

A Sattvic man is a spiritual man. He is endowed with Divya or divine qualities. He has Divya-bhava. He is calm, pure, dispassionate, wise, passionless, egoless, compassionate, kind, pious, devoted. Sattva-Guna predominates in him.

If Tamas predominates in a man, he has Pasu-bhava. He is Pasu or animal. He is endowed with ignorance, error, carelessness, inertia, sloth, etc.

If Rajas predominates in a man, he is a Vira. He has Vira-bhava.

Divya-bhava is the best, the Vira the next best and Pasu the lowest. From being a Pasu, a man rises in this or some other birth to be a Vira. Divya-bhava or Devata-bhava is awakened through Virabhava.

GURU AND DIKSHA (INITIATION)

Yoga should be learnt from a Guru. And this is true all the more in the case of Tantra Yoga. It is the Guru who will recognise the class to which the aspirant belongs and prescribe suitable Sadhana. Now-a-days aspirants have the dangerous and wrong notion of imagining that they are highly qualified to adopt the highest form of Yoga in the very beginning of their Sadhana. This is the reason for the early downfall of the majority of aspirants. This itself shows that he is not yet ready to take to Yoga. The real, qualified aspirant will be humble enough to approach a Guru, surrender himself to the Guru, serve the Guru and learn Yoga from the Guru.

The Guru is none other than the Supreme Divine Mother Herself, descended into the world in order to elevate the aspirants. Deify the Guru. Then only will you be really benefited. Serve him untiringly. He will of his own accord bestow the supreme blessing of Diksha upon you.

Diksha is the giving of the Mantra by the Guru. Initiation gives spiritual knowledge and destroys sin. As one lamp is lit at the flame of another, so the divine Sakti consisting of Mantra is communicated from Guru to the disciple. The disciple fasts, observes Brahmacharya and gets the Mantra from the Guru.

Initiation tears the veil of mystery and enables the disciple to grasp the hidden truth behind scriptural truths. These are generally veiled in mystic language. You cannot understand them by self-study. Self-study will only lead you to greater ignorance. The Guru only will give you, by Diksha, the right perspective in which to study the scriptures. He will flash his torch of Self-realisation on the truth which you will grasp immediately.

SADHANA

Sadhana means any spiritual practice that helps the Sadhaka or aspirant to realise God. Abhyasa and Sadhana are synonymous terms. Sadhana is a means to attain the goal of human life. Without Sadhana no one can achieve the purpose of life. Sadhana is that which produces Siddhi or perfection. It is the means or practice by which the desired end may be attained.

He who is sincere and earnest, who is firm, patient and persevering can make great progress in the spiritual path. The attainment of the goal is possible only by a course of practical spiritual discipline or persistent Sadhana.

Sadhana consists in the exercise and training of the body, senses, the mind and psychic faculties. Sadhana differs in different individuals according to the capacity, temperament and tastes. Sadhya is that which is attained through Sadhana. Sadhya is God or Brahman.

The Sadhana is divided into four classes, according to the physical, mental and moral qualities—Mridu (mild), Madhya (middle), Adhimatruka (higher) and Adhi-matratama (the highest) who is qualified Adhikari for all forms of Yoga.

The means employed are various, such as worship (Puja) exterior or mental; service of Guru; study of scriptures; Tapas (austerity); the Panchatattva Mantra; etc.

Siddhi follows when the mind and senses are controlled, and when the aspirant attains Self-realisation.

The Vasanas and cravings resist. They resist, persist and recur. A Dheera or spiritual hero alone, with patience, perseverance and eternal vigilance, can attain triumph. Pray and attain Mother's Grace. Without Mother's Grace you cannot make an iota of spiritual progress. Sadhana Sakti is Mother's Grace. Guru is Mother's Grace. Sadhana and bodily necessities which a Sadhaka gets are Mother's Grace.

Persist in your Sadhana. You will grow strong and you will have victory over mind, senses and old evil habits ultimately. Do Sadhana with a pure mind and concentration.

Tear off old bad habits. Cultivate new good habits. Eradicate evil traits. Cultivate divine virtues. Steady the mind, strengthen Sadhana-Sakti. Rise above body and mind and attain Self-realisation.

QUALIFICATIONS OF A DISCIPLE

The qualifications of a disciple are purity, faith, devotion, dispassion, truthfulness, control of the senses.

He should be intelligent, a believer in Vedas. He must abstain from injury to all beings. He must be vigilant, diligent, patient and persevering. He must be ever doing good to all.

TANTRA SADHANA

All Sadhana should be done under the direction of a Guru or spiritual teacher.

Mere book-knowledge is not of much use. It is from a Guru that Sadhana and Yoga are learnt.

There is no difference between Guru, Mantra and God. Guru is father, mother and Brahman.

SAVA SADHANA

This is practised by some Vira Sadhakas in the cremation ground. Only the fearless can practise this sort of Sadhana.

A human corpse is laid with its face to the ground. The Sadhaka sits on the back of the body of the dead man. He draws a Yantra on the back and then worships.

If the rite is successful, the head of the corpse turns round and asks the Sadhaka the boon he wants, be it Salvation or some material benefit.

The Devi speaks through the mouth of the dead man.

TAPAS

Tapas is penance or austerity. The Sadhaka shines with spiritual effulgence by the practice of Tapas. Real Tapas is concentration and meditation.

SATTVIC, RAJASIC, TAMASIC TAPAS

That austerity performed by men with the utmost faith, without desire for fruit, harmonised is Sattvic or pure.

That austerity practised with the object of gaining respect, honour and worship and for ostentation, is Rajasic, unstable and fleeting.

That austerity done under a deluded understanding, with self-torture or with the object of destroying another, is declared to be Tamasic or of darkness.

Those men who practise terrific austerities not enjoined by the scriptures, given to hypocrisy and egoism, impelled by the force of lust and attachment, senseless, torturing all the elements in the body and also the Purusha who dwells in the body—know these to be of demoniacal in their resolves.

VRATA

Vrata is performed for purification of the mind. It is a part of Naimittika or voluntary Karma. It is a form of self-restraint.

Hindus observe various kinds of Vratas such as Ekadasi Vrata on the eleventh day of each fortnight, Satyanarayana Vrata in honour of Lord Narayana, Varalakshmi Vrata in honour of Goddess Maha Lakshmi, Anantapadmanabha Vrata, Savitri Vrata, Janmashtami Vrata, Chandrayana Vrata, Krischra Vrata, Pradosha Vrata. Some fast on Ekadasi or Pradosha days, to propitiate Lord Vishnu and Lord Siva respectively. Some fast on Sundays to propiriate the Sun. Some fast on Mondays to propitiate Lord Siva. On Nirjala Edadasi they do not take even a drop of water. On Satyanarayana Vrata day they fast and do Puja or worship of Lord Vishnu. The priest reads Satyanarayana Katha. In Sivaratri Vrata in honour of Lord Siva, they fast, keep vigil and do worship of Lord Siva. On Sri Krishna Janmashtami day, the devotees fast and celebrate the birthday of Lord Krishna. All Vratas aim at purifying the heart, controlling the senses and cultivating devotion to the Lord. The worldly people are always busy in earning money and doing various kinds of work. At least during these days of Vrata, they have the opportunity to introspect, to worship, to do Japa and intense meditation, to study holy scriptures and to practise self-analysis. Chandrayana Vrata and Krischra Vrata are observed for expiation of sins and to purify the heart.

Each Vrata has its peculiarities. Certain features are common to different Vratas. The aspirant observes Brahmacharya or sexual continence, fasts or takes milk and fruits or light diet. No fish or meat is taken.

SIDDHI

Siddhi is perfection. Siddha is one who has attained perfection or Self-realisation. Siddhi is attained by Sadhana. Siddhi literally means success, achievement, attainment and fruition of all kinds.

One may attain Siddhi in speech, Siddhi in Mantra, Siddhi in Yoga, etc.

The eight major Siddhis are Anima (the power of becoming small), Mahima (the power of becoming great), Laghima (the power of becoming light), Garima (the power of becoming heavy), Prapti (the power of reaching anywhere, the power to approach distant things even to moon, to reach it with tip of finger), Prakamya (the power of having all desires realised), Ishitva (lordship), Vashitva (the power to command all or the perfect control over elements).

The minor Siddhis are Doora Darshan (clairvoyance), Doora Sravan (Clairaudience), Kama-rupa (assuming any form you like), Parakaya-pravesha (entering into another body, or animating a dead body and entering into it by transforming his soul), Iccha Mrityu (death at his will), Trikala-Jnana (knowledge of past, present and future), Kaya-vyuha (taking as many bodies as the Yogi likes to exhaust all his Karmas in one life). He gets the knowledge of his past life. He gets knowledge of the cluster of stars and planets. The Yogi rises in the air and leaves the ground (Vayu Siddhi).

The greatest of all Siddhis is liberation or Moksha, freedom from the cycle of births and deaths and union with Parabrahman or Supreme Being.

The aspirant should not run after Siddhis as he will get a downfall. He may misuse the powers. He should ignore them as they are obstacles in the spiritual path, and reach the goal directly.

RULES FOR THE WORSHIP OF PARA-SAKTI

I shall tell you the rules for the worship of Para-Sakti, which will give you both wisdom and salvation. Hear with attention.

The worship of Para-Sakti is said to be of two kinds; external worship and mental worship. Of these, again, external worship is further subdivided into Vaidika and Tantrika worship. The former is meant for the followers of the Vedas and the latter for the Tantrikas.

In this way the worship for all the Devatas is formally prescribed. Those who do not follow the prescribed ways of Devata-worship, will rush to ruin.

For Sakti-Puja the same procedure is adopted, in many respects, as in the case of Sivalinga worship. Here also we have Asana (seating of the Deity), invocation, Arghya, Padya, Achamana, bathing, dressing,

---

ornamentation, offering scents, flowers, illumination, offering sweets, fruits and other articles of food, drinks, garlands, sandal-paste, prostrations, etc. Here also the Deity is invoked and revoked after the Puja in one's heart. Of the Mantras in worship, the Matrika Mantra which is the mother of all Mantras should be pronounced. Without the Matrika the Mantras do not exist.

And, the Matrika Mantra uttered by the worshipper, is of three kinds. It varies according to the degree of spiritual evolution of the worshipper, and is divided into gross, fine and superfine. And this Matrika Mantra should be learnt from a Satguru, after initiation. It can never be learnt merely from Sastras or scriptures.

Every Mantra has four important places in the human constitution—Para, Pasyanti, Madhyama and Vaikhari. Of these Para is the Matra in its extra-superfine sound-origin in the Muladhara centre of the human system. The form of this inchoate sound is discernible only to advanced spiritual students who have become Jivanmuktas—who have entered the portals of Immortality, but still subsist in their bodily state as mortal men. Pasyanti is that form of this inchoate Mantric sound perceived by Yogis only in the part around the navel in the human body. When the same Mantric sound is heard in the heart, it is called Madhyama. The fourth or final stage of the Mantric sound becomes audible as it enters the neck and comes out of the throat and lips. Then it is called Vaikhari. It is now in its gross form and can be heard by others too, besides the producer of the sound. If the Mantra is uttered in its superfine state in the Para and Pasyanti stages, Mantric worship is said to be of the superfine type. If it is uttered in its Madhyama form, the worship is said to be of the fine type; and in its audible form, the worship is said to be of the gross form.

A person who is fit to do mental worship, should abandon external worship, and should not waste his time and energies in performing the latter.

The internal worship of Devi too, is further classified into two forms: one located or fixed in some part of the internal constitution; and another not so fixed or located. The latter is the superior mode of worship.

The localised internal worship of Sakti may be in any one of the centres, from Muladhara to Ajna and the unlocalised internal worship is established purely in one's consciousness, in the Samvit part of the human system. In the former the Sadhaka worships Devi or the Divine Mother in a special form indicated by the Matrika Mantra or seed-letters while in the latter, he loses himself in the conception of the Devi and becomes one with Her. The worship should be performed with intense devotion and in consonance with the instructions of the preceptor.

Samvit means Para-Sakti, and in fact not anything else. Therefore, O Great Munis of Naimisha, Para-Sakti should be always worshipped. (In this case Puja or worship really means Atmic Bliss of self-identity with Para-Sakti.)

Whatever appears different from pure consciousness is considered to be Samsara in which souls are entangled.

Therefore, in order to destroy the ignorance caused by Samsara, one must worship Para-Sakti as the universal Witness, the Soul of all things, and quite free from all kinds of attributes of form and name, other limiting conditions and qualities belonging to the universe.

The wise one should therefore first worship with great faith the blessed Para-Sakti of the nature of pure, unconditioned consciousness by the Matrika Mantra (Hreem) signifying that consciousness.

He must avoid all forms and details recommended in the earlier part of this discourse, must identify himself with the One Supreme Sublime perfect consciousness of Para-Sakti by constant meditation. Then he must destroy the duality too, as between him, the worshipper and Para-Sakti, the Divine Mother worshipped by him.

That kind of Puja of Para-Sakti wherein the Sadhaka by his own identification with the all-embracing divine consciousness, devoutly worships and perceives Mahesvara by direct Self-experience will surely gain him the supreme end of life.

Thus the method of the Puja of Para-Sakti as directed in the Veda has been told to you by me. Therefore you all proceed forthwith to worship Her in the manner described with the greatest joy.

Divine worship is of three kinds: Siva-Puja, Devi-Puja, and the worship of the Bhaktas. Each of these three is subdivided into Vedic worship and Tantric worship. Vedic worship is divided into three types: the gross form, the subtle form and the Absolute form. That is to say external worship of God through images, mental worship of God, and finally identification of oneself with God or Goddess.

BHUTA SUDDHI

Bhuta Suddhi is an important Tantric rite. It means purification of five elements of which the body is composed.

The Sadhaka dissolves the sinful body and makes a new Deva body. He infuses into the body the life of the Devi.

The Sadhaka imagines that Kundalini is aroused and that one element is absorbed into the other and so on, until all are absorbed in Brahman.

NYASA

Nyasa is a very important and powerful Tantric rite. It is placing of the tips of the fingers of the right hand on various parts of the body, accompanied by Mantra.

KAVACHA

The one Brahman is here invoked by different names in order to protect different parts of the body. Parabrahman is thought of as in the Sahasrara Padma in the head. The Supreme Lord is the object of meditation in the heart. The protector of the world, Vishnu, is invoked to protect the throat, so that the aspirant may utter the Mantras of his Ishta Devata.

May the Supreme Brahman protect the head,
May the Supreme Lord protect the heart,
May Vishnu protect the throat,
May the Lord protect the face,
May the Lord protect my hands,
May He protect my feet,
May He protect my body in all its parts always.

The Mantra is written on birch-bark and encased in a golden ball and worn round the neck, or on the right arm.

The wearer gets protection and attains all kinds of powers.

MUDRA

Mudra is ritual of manual gestures. Mudra gives pleasure to the Devatas. There are 108 Mudras. In welcoming (Avahana) the Devata an appropriate gesture is made. In making offering (Arghya) Matsya Mudra is made. The right hand is placed on the back of the left and the two thumbs are extended finlike on each side of the hands. Similarly there are Mudras for the various acts done during the Puja.

THE PANCHA TATTVA

The Pancha Tattva is essential for the worship of Sakti. The Pancha Tattvas are wine (Madya), meat (Mamsa), fish (Matsya), parched cereal (Mudra) and sexual union (Maithuna). As they all commence with the letter M, they are vulgarly called Pancha-ma-kara or five M's. The Pancha Tattvas stand for drinking, eating and propagation. The Pancha Tattvas, the five elements of worship destroy great sins, Maha-pataka-nasanam.

The Pancha Tattvas have not always their literal meaning. The meaning differs according as they refer to the Tamasic (Pasu), Rajasic (Vira) or Sattvic (Divya) Sadhanas respectively.

Wine may be wine; or it may be coconut water or it may mean God-intoxication or the intoxicating knowledge of Brahman or the Absolute. Wine is a symbol to denote the Supreme, eternal Bliss of Yoga knowledge, or knowledge of Atman (Atma-jnana).

The union of Siva and Sakti in the upper brain centre known as Sahasrara or thousand-petalled lotus is Maithuna.

Mamsa (meat) is the act by which the aspirant consecrates all his actions to the Lord.

Matsya (fish) is that Sattvic knowledge by which the Sadhaka sympathises with the pleasure and pain of all beings.

Mudra is the act of abandoning all associations with evil which leads to bondage.

Wine is fire; flesh is air; fish is water; cereal is earth; sexual union is ether.

Milk, ghee, honey are all substitutes for wine. Salt, ginger, sesamum, white beans, garlic are substitutes for meat. White brinjal, red radish, *masur* (a kind of grain) and red sesamum are substitutes for fish. Paddy, rice, wheat and grain are Mudra. Offering of flowers with the hands formed with a particular Mudra is Maithuna.

The Sadhaka thinks that he has got a Deva body. This is Bhuta-Suddhi. Various Nyasas are performed. Mental worship is performed of the Devi who is thought of as being in red raiment seated on a red lotus. Her dark body is like rain-cloud. Her forehead is shining with the light of the crescent moon. Japa of Mantra is then done. Thereupon there is external worship.

Sexual intercourse by a man with a woman who is not lawful to him is a sin. The Vaidika Dharma is very strict on this point. It forbids not merely actual Maithuna but Ashtanga or eightfold Maithuna namely Smaranam (thinking upon it), Kirtanam (talking of it), Keli (play with women), Prekshanam (making eyes at women),

Guhya-bhashanam (talking in private with women), Sankalpa (wish or resolve for sexual union), Adhyavasaya (determination towards it), Kriyanishpatti (actual accomplishment of the sexual act).

A Tantric can have copulation with his wife. He calls his wife his Sakti. Wife is a house-goddess Griha-lakshmi or Griha-devata united to her husband by the sacramental Samskara of marriage. She should not be regarded as an object of enjoyment. She is his partner in life (Ardhangini). The union of a man and his wife is a veritable sacred scriptural rite.

UPACHARA

The materials used or acts done in Puja are called Upachara. They are sixteen in number.

1. Asana (seating of the image).

2. Svagata (welcoming of the Devata).

3. Padya (water for washing the feet).

4. Arghya [(offering—Samanya (general) and Visesha (special)].

5. Achamana (water for sipping and cleansing the lips).

6. Madhuparka (honey, ghee, milk and curd).

7. Snana (water for bath).

8. Vastra (cloth).

9. Abharana (ornaments).

10. Gandha (perfume).

11. Pushpa (flowers).

12. Dhupa (incense).

13. Dipa (light).

14. Naivedya (food); Tambula (betel-nut).

15. Neerajana (waving of camphor).

16. Vandana or Namak Kriya (prostration, prayer).

YANTRA

Yantra takes the place of the image. It is an object of worship. It subdues lust, anger and other sufferings of the Jiva. Hence it is called Yantra.

The Yantra is a diagram, drawn on paper. It is engraved on a metal also. A Yantra is appropriated to a specific Devata only. Various Yantras are peculiar to each Devata. They are of various designs according to the object of worship. Yantra is the body of the Devata.

All Yantras have a common edging called Bhupura. They have a quadrangular figure with four doors which encloses and separates the Yantra from the external world.

The Sadhaka first meditates upon the Devata or Deity and then arouses the Devata in himself. He then communicates the Divine persence thus aroused to the Yantra. When the Devi has been invoked into the Yantra by the appropriate Mantra, the vital airs (Prana) of the Devata are infused therein by the Pranapratishtha ceremony. The Devata is thereby installed in the Yantra.

CHAKRA PUJA

The worshippers sit in a circle (Chakra) men and women alternately. The Sakti (Bhairavi) sits on the left of the Sadhaka (Bhairava). The Lord of the Chakra

(Chakra-swamin or Chakresvara) sits with his Sakti (Chakresvari) in the centre.

All eat, drink and worship together. There is no distinction of caste.

There are various kinds of Chakras such as the Vira, Raja, Deva and Maha. Each Chakra bestows various fruits on the worshippers therein.

MANASIC PUJA

Manasic Puja is more powerful than external Puja with flowers, etc. Arjuna thought that Bhima was not doing any kind of worship. He was proud of his external worship to Lord Siva. He offered *Bel*-leaves. But Bhima offered to Lord Siva mentally the *Bel*-leaves of all the *Bel*-trees of the whole world. He was doing Manasic Puja of Lord Siva. The attendants of Lord Siva were not able to remove the *Bel*-leaves offered by Bhima from the head of Lord Siva. Arjuna once saw a large band of people carrying baskets of *Bel*-leaves. He thought within himself that these leaves should be those offered by him to Lord Siva and questioned them thus, "Brothers, wherefrom do you carry these *Bel*-leaves?" They replied, "O Arjuna, these leaves were offered to our Lord Siva by Bhima through his Manasic Puja." Arjuna was struck with wonder. He came to know that Manasic Puja was more powerful than the external worship and that Bhima was a better devotee than him. His pride was destroyed. He became very humble.

Manasic Puja can be done by advanced students. Beginners should certainly do worship with flowers, sandal-paste, incense, etc. You will have more concentration when you do Manasic Puja. Mentally enthrone the Devata in Simhasana set with diamonds, pearls, emeralds, etc. Offer Him a seat. Apply sandal-paste to His forehead and body. Offer Arghyam, Madhuparka and various sorts of flowers, clothes. Offer various kinds of fruits, sweetmeats and Maha Naivedyam. Offer to the Lord the fruits of the whole world. Do not be miserly even in Manasic Puja. In Manasic Puja one man offered only one stale plantain fruit and handful of gram. A miserable miserly man! Even in Manasic Puja he could not be generous and liberal. In the end mentally repeat: "Whatever action I do with the body, by speech, by the mind, by the senses, by the intellect or by my own nature, I offer all of them to the Supreme Lord." This will purify your heart and remove the taint of expectation of reward.

BHAVA IN WORSHIP

Bhava is mental attitude. Spiritual mental attitude is divine Bhava. It is Bhava that counts much in meditation and worship.

There is delay in the vision of God because you do not have the Bhillini-bhava or the Bhava of Dhanna Bhagat. Bhillini offered only the fruits which she tasted before she offered them to Lord Rama. Lord Rama was very much pleased. Dhanna Bhagat of Punjab gave only a little cooked vegetable to the Lord. The Lord was highly delighted. God does not want golden temples and rich presents. He wants only your devoted heart. He is immensely pleased with a little flower, or fruit or a little water, if it is offered with intense devotion, faith and love.

You will have to cultivate the divine Bhava again and again through love, faith, devotion, Japa, prayer, meditation and service to the Lord. Cultivate the nine modes of devotion and you will be rich with divine Bhava.

There are four kinds of Bhava in worship. They are Brahma-bhava, Dhyana-bhava, the Bhava that is generated during Japa, singing hymns and prayer, and Puja-bhava.

The realisation that everything is Brahman, "I am Brahman," that the individual soul and the Supreme Soul are one, and that nothing but Brahman exists is Brahma-bhava or the highest state. Sri Dattatreya, Sri Sankara, Sri Yajnavalkya had this Supreme Bhava. For such a realised sage there is neither worshipper nor worshipped, neither Yoga nor Puja, nor Dharana, Dhyana, Japa, Stava or Vrata.

Constant meditation by the Yoga-process upon the Devata in the heart is the Dhyana-bhava. Japa, hymns and prayer is still lower. Puja-bhava is the lowest of all Bhavas. Puja-bhava is generated out of the dualistic notions of worshipper and worshipped, the servant and the Lord.

You cannot have the Brahma-bhava all at once. You will have to slowly ascend the ladder of Bhava—from Puja-bhava to Dhyana-bhava and from Dhyana-bhava to Brahma-bhava. The heart must be purified thoroughly through Japa, hymns, prayer and meditation.

MANTRA YOGA

Mantra Yoga is an exact science. *Mananat trayate iti mantrah:* by the Manana or constant thinking or recollection of which one is released from the round of births and deaths is Mantra.

Mantra is Divinity. Mantra and its presiding Devata are one. Mantra is divine power. The repetition of the Mantra removes the dirt of the mind such as lust, anger, greed, etc.

The rhythmical vibrations of its sounds regulate the unsteady vibrations of the sheaths of the aspirant, and transform him into divinity. Mantra-siddhi is the ability to make a Mantra efficacious and to obtain its fruit.

When the Mantra-sakti is awakened by Sadhana, the presiding Devata appears; when perfect Mantra-siddhi is attained, the Devata is revealed.

Sabda or sound is the Guna of Akasa or ether. It is not produced by Akasa, but manifests in it.

A Mantra is composed of certain letters arranged in definite sequence of sound of which the letters are the representative signs. Mantra must be intoned in the proper way according to Svara (rhythm) and Varna (sound). Sabda is the manifestation of the Chit-sakti itself.

Every Mantra has a Rishi who gave it to the world, a Matra, a Devata, the Bija or seed which gives it a special power, the Sakti and the Kilakam or pillar.

Constant repetition of the Mantra with faith, devotion and purity augments the Sakti or power of the Sadhaka, purifies and awakens the Mantra-chaitanya latent in the Mantra and bestows Mantra-siddhi on the Sadhaka; illumination, freedom, peace, eternal bliss and Immortality follow.

The Mantra is awakened from its sleep through the Sadhana-sakti of the aspirant. The Mantra is a mass of radiant Tejas or energy. Mantra awakens supernatural powers. Mantra produces harmony. It has the power of releasing the cosmic and the supercosmic consciousness.

JAPA OF MANTRA

Repeat the Mantra verbally for some time, in a whisper for some time, and mentally for some time. The mind wants variety. It gets disgusted with any monotonous practice. The mental repetition is very powerful. It is termed Manasika Japa. The verbal repetition is called Vaikhari Japa. Repetition in a whisper or humming is termed Upamshu Japa. Even mechanical repetition of Japa without any Bhava has a great purifying effect on the heart or the mind. The feeling will come later on when the process of mental process goes on.

The loud Japa shuts out all worldly sounds. There is no break of Japa here. This is one advantage in loud Japa. Manasika Japa is difficult for ordinary people, and break may come in the mind after a while. Whenever sleep tries to overpower you when doing Japa at night, take the Mala in your hand and roll the beads. This will put a check to sleep. This is another advantage in loud Japa. Repeat the Mantra loudly. Give up Manasika Japa at this time. The Mala will remind you of the stoppage of Japa. When sleep comes in, stand up and do the Japa.

Sandilya says in Sandilya Upanishad: "The Vaikhari Japa (loud pronunciation) gives the reward as stated in the Vedas, while the Upamsu Japa (whispering or humming), which cannot be heard by anyone, gives a reward a thousand times more than the Vaikhari; the Manasika Japa (mental Japa) gives a reward a crore times more than the Vaikhari Japa."

Do Japa in the throat or Kantha for one year. This is verbal Japa or Vaikhari Japa in a loud tone. Do it in the heart or Hridaya for two years. This is mental or Manasika Japa. Do it in the Nabhi or navel for one year. This kind of Japa is associated with the breath.

When you advance in practice, every pore in the skin, every hair on the body, will repeat the Mantra forcibly. The whole system will be charged with the powerful vibration of the Mantra. You will be ever in the Prema or Love of the Devata. You will experience muscular twitchings and will shed profuse tears of Ananda. You will be in an exalted Divine mood. You will get inspiration, revelation, ecstasy, insight, intuition and Parama-ananda. You will compose inspiring poems. You will have various Siddhis, Divine Aisvarya, treasures of heaven.

Repeat the Name constantly. This will lead quite easily to control of mind. Do it with absolute Sraddha (faith). Do it with Antarika-prema (love from the bottom of your heart) and Anuraga (intense affection). You must intensely feel for the long, painful seperation from the Lord. Tears must flow profusely from your eyes. This is Viraha-agni. When you repeat the Name remember that the Devata is dwelling in the chambers of your heart, in the Anahata Chakra, in the midst of a blazing light.

PURASCHARANA

The mode of repetition of a Mantra with feeling and in a particular manner, a definite number of times, with right observances until a fixed number of Japa is reached, in order to obtain substantial benefit out of the Mantra, is called Purascharana.

The Practitioner of Purascharana of a Mantra should take vegetables, fruits, milk, roots and tubers, curd, barley, Havishya (rice cooked along with ghee, sugar and milk, and which has been offered to God) or he may live on pure Bhiksha alone.

Any holy place of pilgrimage and holy place on the banks of holy rivers, caves, tops of hills and mountains, confluence of rivers, huge holy forests, below the Asvattha tree—all these are recommended as places fit for doing Purascharana.

The Sadhaka should sit facing either the east or the north, during Japa. During the night time, he may sit facing the north only. One should bathe three times a day, and if it is impossible, he may take bath at least twice, or even once, according to his convenience and prevailing circumstances. An advanced aspirant can use any Mala or he may not use the Mala at all. It all depends upon the stage of evolution in which one is. Padma, Siddha, Svastika, Sukha, or Vira Asana is recommended for Japa. Cotton cloth, blanket, silk or tiger skin should be used as seat which will bring Saubhagya, Jnana and Siddhi.

Abstracting the mind from all worldly objects, being merged in the inner meaning of the Mantra, one should repeat the Mantra, neither very quickly nor too slowly. The Mantra should be repeated as many lakhs of times as there are letters contained in the Mantra.

The number of Japa done during each day should be constant, and should not vary day by day. Every day after finishing the Japa, Ahutis of Ghee or oblations of the Charus that are prescribed, equal in number to one-tenth of the Japa done should be offered in the sacred fire. Or else, this may also be done at the end of each lakh of Japa.

When the required number of Japa is over, oblations equal in number to one-tenth of the total Japa done, should be offered in Yajna, uttering the same Mantra with each offering or Ahuti.

In case, one is unable to perform Homa and observe its restrictions, he can worship the Deity, do, in addition to the total Japa already done, further Japa equal in number to one-tenth, and feed Brahmins and Mahatmas afterwards.

Sleeping on the bare ground, celibacy, worship of the Deity three times a day, prayer to the Deity, faith in the Mantra, bath three times every day, abandoning of oil-bath, are to be observed strictly as vows during the Mantra-sadhana.

The Sadhaka should not sit placing one leg on the other, and he should not touch his feet with hands. Concentration of the mind on the Mantra and its meaning is very essential at all times. Japa should not be done when walking here and there or looking this side and that side. The Upasaka should never be engaged in other activities even in mind, and should not be murmuring, grumbling, etc., or covering the face with any kind of garment.

Brightness, clearness and tranquillity of mind, contentment, dispassion towards sense-objects, will dawn on Mantra-siddhi, if the Purascharana is done without any selfish motive or desire behind it. The aspirant should not do Purascharana for any petty selfish end. Sakama-upasana will not bring to him real spiritual knowledge and experience or inner strength. Japa should be done with an aspiration to obtain the grace of the Deity and realise the Deity. The best Purascharana is that which is done for self-purification and Atma-sakshatkara. After this, the Purascharana that is done will bring Sakshatkara or realisation of the Deity.

BIJA-AKSHARAS

A Bija-Akshara is a seed-letter. It is a very powerful Mantra. Every Devata has his or her own Bija-Akshara. The greatest of all Bija-Aksharas is Om or Pranava, for it is the symbol of the Parabrahman, or the Paramatman Himself. Om contains within itself all the other Bija-Aksharas. Om is the general sound or the common seed from which all the particular sounds or secondary seeds proceed. The letters of the alphabet are only emanations from Om which is the root of all sounds and letters. There is no Mantra superior to or greater than Om. Om, as it is pronounced ordinarily, is an outward gross form of the real subtle inaudible state of sound which is called the Amatra or the immeasurable fourth transcendental state. As the various Devatas are the aspects or forms of the One Supreme Being, so the various Bija-Aksharas or Bija-Mantras are so many aspects or forms of the Supreme Bija or Mantra, viz., Om. Even the letters 'A', 'U' and 'M' do not really give the transcendental or original state of sound. Even this triliteral sound is only an expression or manifestation of the highest primal Dhvani or Vibration. The transcendental sound of Om is heard only by Yogis and not by the ordinary ear. In the correct pronunciation of Om the sound proceeds from the navel, with a deep and harmonious vibration, and gradually manifests itself by stages at the upper part of the nostrils where the Anusvara or the Chandrabindu is sounded.

Generally a Bija-Mantra consists of a single letter. Sometimes it constitutes several syllables. For example, the Bija-Mantra 'Kam' has a single letter with the Anusvara or the Chandrabindu, Nada and Bindu are blended together. Some Bija-Mantras are made up of compound letters, such as the Mantra 'Hreem'. The Bija-Mantras have a significant inner meaning and often do not convey any meaning on their face. Their meaning is subtle, mystic. The form of the Bija-Mantra is the form of the Devata signified by it.

The Bijas of the five Mahabhutas or great elements, i.e., of the Devatas or the presiding intelligences of the elements, viz., Ether, Air, Fire, Water and Earth, are respectively Ham, Yam, Ram, Vam and Lam. The meanings of a few Bija-Mantras are given here, to serve as examples.

OM

Om consists of three letters: A, U, and M. It signifies the three periods of time, the three states of consciousness, the entire existence. A is the waking state or Virat and Visva. U is the dreaming state of Hiranyagarbha or Taijasa. M is the sleeping state or Isvara and Prajna. Study the Mandukyopanishad in detail in order to understand the meaning of Om.

HAUM

In this Mantra, Ha is Siva. Au is Sadasiva. The Nada and Bindu mean that which dispel sorrow. With this Mantra Lord Siva should be worshipped.

DUM

Here Da means Durga. U means to protect. Nada means the mother of the universe. Bindu signifies action (worship or prayer). This is the Mantra of Durga.

KREEM

With this Mantra Kalika should be worshipped. Ka is Kali. Ra is Brahma. Ee is Mahamaya. Nada is mother of the universe. Bindu is the dispeller of sorrow.

HREEM

This is the Mantra of Mahamaya or Bhuvanesvari. Ha means Siva. Ra is Prakriti. Ee means Mahamaya. Nada is the Mother of the universe. Bindu means the dispeller of sorrow.

SHREEM

This is the Mantra of Mahalakshmi. Sha is Mahalakshmi. Ra means wealth. Ee means satisfaction or contentment. Nada is Apara or the manifested Brahman or Isvara. Bindu means the dispeller of sorrow.

AIM

This is the Bija-Mantra of Sarasvati. Ai means Sarasvati. Bindu means the dispeller of sorrow. This is also Guru-Bija.

KLEEM

This is the Kamabija. Ka means the Lord of desire (Kamadeva). Ka may also mean Krishna. La means Indra. Ee means contentment or satisfaction. Nada and Bindu mean that which bring happiness and dispel sorrow.

HOOM

In this Mantra, Ha is Siva. U is Bhairava. Nada is the Supreme. Bindu means the dispeller of sorrow. This is threefold Bija of Varma or armour (coat of mail).

GAM

This is the Ganesa-Bija. Ga means Ganesa. Bindu means the dispeller of sorrow.

GLAUM

This is also a Mantra of Ganesa. Ga means Ganesa. La means that which pervades. Au means lustre or brilliance. Bindu means the dispeller of sorrow.

KSHRAUM

This is the Bija of Narasimha. Ksha is Narasimha. Ra is Brahman. Au means 'with teeth pointing upwards'. Bindu means the dispeller of sorrow.

There are, like these, many other Bija-Mantras which signify various Devatas. 'Vyaam' is the Bija of Vyasa-Mantra, `Brum' is the Bija of Brihaspati Mantra, `Raam' of Rama-Mantra. Aim Kleem Sauh are the Bija-Mantras of Bala Tripurasundari. Aim Hreem Kleem Chamundaayai Vicche are the Bija-Mantras of Chamundesvari.

Bijas have no meaning according to the ordinary use of language. Their meaning is the own form or Svarupa of the particular Devata whose Mantra they are. They are a form of the subtle power as creative Dhvani.

Each letter, syllable and Mantra is a form of Brahman. The primary Mantra in the worship of any Deva or Devi is known as the Mula-Mantra (root-Mantra). All letters are forms of Sakti as sound powers.

The Bija-Mantras can be recited by persons who have knowledge of Sanskrit and know the proper intonation.

SRI VIDYA

Sri Vidya is the great Mantra of Tripurasundari or Bhuvanesvari or Mahamaya. It is also called the Panchadasi or the Panchadasakshari, for it is formed of fifteen letters. In its developed form it consists of sixteen letters and is called Shodasi or the Shodasakshari. The aspirant should directly get initiation of this Mantra from a Guru, and should not start reciting of this Mantra for himself or doing Japa of it, of his own accord. This is a very powerful Mantra. So it is imperative that it should be got directly from a Guru who has got Siddhi of this Mantra.

The general rule is that this Mantra (Sri Vidya) should be repeated after one's passing through certain stages of self-purification through other Mantras. In the beginning a Purascharana of Ganesa Mantra should be done. Then Purascharana of Gayatri-Mantra, Maha Mrityunjaya-Mantra and Durga-Mantra (Vaidika or Tantrika) have to be done. After this the Panchadasakshari and the Shodasakshari have to be taken up for Japa.

The Sri Vidya should not be repeated by those who are not well acquainted with this. Only those who have a very good knowledge of the Sanskrit language and who have been directly initiated by a Guru (who has Mantra-Siddhi) can take up the Japa of the Sri Vidya. Others should not approach this Mantra and should do only Japa of their own Ishta Mantras which are very easy to pronounce and remember.

The Sri Chakra or Sri Yantra is the Yantra of Lalita or Tripurasundari, the Devata of Sri Vidya. Every Devata has his or her Yantra. Lalita is the supreme Sakti aspect of Brahman.

The Chakras extend from the point or Bindu called Sarvanandamaya; the Supreme Siva-Sakti in the centre to the outermost section of the Chakras the Bhupura which is called Trailokyamohana.

The aim of the Sadhaka of Lalita is to realise his identity first with the Yantra and Mantra and then with Lalita or Tripura, the Mahasakti who is the creator and director of the universe.

If Para-Sakti was not united with Para-Siva, She could not produce the universe which is within Herself. Therefore the world cannot be created by Siva alone nor by Sakti alone. It is by both of them all the Tattvas are produced.

Without Siva there is no Devi. Without Devi there is no Siva. There is no difference between Siva and Sakti.

In the external form of worship the Sri Chakra is worshipped. Yantra is inscribed on the Bhurja leaf of gold or other metallic plates. Mantras are repeated with gestures, postures, waving of light or Arati and offerings of incense, Naivedya or various sorts of food or Prasad.

Sri Chakra is the highest point or acme to which Yoga practices can lead. When you attain perfection in Sri Vidya, there is nothing more left for you to gain by the practice of Yoga. Sri Chakra with forty-three triangles is the mansion of the Devi. In the Sri Chakra (Nagara) in the centre between the seventeenth and eighteenth walls, is the seat of Vishnu; between the sixteenth and seventeenth is that of Brahma; between the fourteenth and the fifteenth is that of Indra and other Lokapalas (protectors of the world). All these reside (in the respective places) for the sake of worshipping Devi. The Devi-Bhagavata Purana says: "Brahma, Vishnu, Indra, Varuna, Yama, Vayu, Agni, Kubera, Tvashta, Pusha, Asvins, Bhaga, Adityas, Vasus, Rudras, Visvadevas, Marudganas, all these meditate on Devi, the cause of creation, preservation and destruction.

Outside and beyond the countless myriads of the world's systems, in the centre of the Ocean of Nectar, more than a thousand crores in extent, in the Gem Island (Ratnadvipa), a hundred crores in area, the lamp of the world, there is the supreme city of Sri Vidya, three lacs of Yojanas in height and adorned with twenty-five walls representing the twenty-five Tattvas.

SYMPOSIUM ON SAKTI

1

TANTRA YOGA

(Sri P.C. Diwanji)

The fact that in the early Upanishads there are no references to the six Chakras, the Kanda, the four Pithas, the Vahnisthana, the Kundalini, the process of rousing it and the development of its latent powers, which are said in some of the Upanishads of the Smarta class such as the Jabala Darsana, Trisikha-Brahman, Varaha, Yoga-Chudamani and several others to enable the Yogis to perform miracles, leads to the inference that no beginning had been made in that early age of the kind of Yoga known as the Tantra Yoga or Kundalini Yoga. That inference is supported by the facts that the processes of rousing of the Kundalini, and the development of the Chakras and the union of the Kundalini which is said to be a microcosmic form of the Sakti of the Lord Siva, with the Linga (symbol) of the Lord located in the portion of the head above the forehead, were dependent upon the Hatha Yoga, the Yoga of the Prana and the Apana, as explained in detail in some of the later Upanishads and in the specific treatises on that Yoga such as the Siva-Samhita, Gheranda Samhita and Hathayoga-Pradipika and in those on the Tantra Yoga such as the Mahanirvana-Tantra, Kularnava-Tantra and others, and that the process of Pranayama itself was in the experimental stage in the age of those early Upanishads. It was in a later age that the Yogis who set a higher value on Self-realisation and the peace of mind resulting therefrom progressed from the Hatha Yoga to what is

----

called Raja Yoga in the above special treatises, and those who valued more the acquisition of miraculous powers progressed from the same Yoga to the Tantra Yoga, which lays special empahsis on the development of the powers latent in the six Chakras from Muladhara to Ajna.

2

SAKTI IN CREATION

(Swami Sadananda)

As long as we live and move in this universe, we are aware of a Power or Sakti that sustains and motivates it. If we think of what the universe itself is, we shall find that it is not as it first appears. When we speak of the universe, we speak of the beings that inhabit and constitute it—men, birds, beasts, plants and minerals. We find the universe consisting of tangible and also intangible things. Not only do we find concrete matter but also such things as heat, light, sound, magnetism and electricity. Nay, more, we find in the universe, hatred, fear, avarice, greed, jealousy, etc., and also love, mercy, compassion, charity, generosity, etc. We also find in the universe the sense of right and wrong, the sense of the beautiful and the sense of the true and the good. We speak of some things as perishable and others are imperishable. When we do so, we mean that some things go out of our sight and some do not. In truth, what looks like matter is really found to be energy or force.

Now it is possible to group all these and arrange them in such a way that our view of the universe may be clear and also complete. That has been done by our ancients who have given us the Sankhya and Yoga philosophies. They have started from the five primordial elements which they call Pancha-Bhutas, viz., Prithvi or earth, Apas or water, Tejas or fire, Vayu or wind and Akasa or ether. The whole of creation in the concrete forms is made of the combinations in different proportions of these five elements. Beyond these elements, there are five Tanmatras corresponding to the five elements. They are Sabda (sound), Sparsa (sense of touch), Rupa (form), Rasa (taste) and Gandha (smell).

Having disposed of the concrete part of creation in this fashion, our ancients have dealt with the equipment found in individual Jivas which enables them to recognise and make use of these concrete objects in the universe. This equipment consists of the five Jnana-Indriyas and the five Karma-Indriyas. The former are the windows of consciousness and the latter are the instruments of action. To make use of these Indriyas, a separate entity is needed, and that is spoken of as Manas or the mind.

The mind also is regarded by our ancients as an instrument to be used by the Jiva. According to Patanjali's system of Yoga, the Jiva creates for its own special use a special mind and a special set of Indriyas so that the experience which that particular Jiva seeks for in the universe may be gained. For example, a buffalo has to create a buffalo's mind so that it may have the buffalo's experience of the universe. Man has to get a different experience. The Jiva of the eagle creates a special eye (one of the Jnana-Indriyas) so that it can see much more than the human eye. Thus, according to Patanjali, there are six Aviseshas or common things and sixteen Viseshas or special things. The common things are (1) Ahankara— the sense of 'I-ness', and (2) the five Tanmatras, viz., Sabda, Sparsa, Rupa, Rasa and Gandha. The Viseshas or special things are (1) the Manas (or Buddhi), (2) the ten Indriyas, and (3) the five Bhutas (elements).

ORDER OF CREATION

There is an order of Creation mentioned in our scriptures which, if understood, will give us a clear idea of what position and status should be assigned to the objects and forces we see in the universe. First of all Sakti emanated from Purusha, the Supreme Being. This Sakti is called either Pradhana, or Prakriti, or Alinga. The last name means "without any distinguishing mark." The meaning is that as pure undifferentiated Sakti or Power, it is not possible to recognise even its existence. That is the Para-Sakti or Supreme Power. It can be called Atma-Sakti or Chit-Sakti. From the Pradhana (or Prakriti or Alinga) came the Mahat or Linga Matra (only the Linga). It is the manifestation of pure Sattvic force in the Alinga.

There are three Gunas—Sattva, Rajas and Tamas. The first is detected by Prakasa or brilliance, the second by movement and the third by its power of resistance. In Mahat the qualities of Rajas and Tamas are hidden and only the Sattva shows itself. Therefore, we cannot find in Mahat—which is also Cosmic Intelligence—any Chalana or change or modification; nor can we find resistance. It does not refuse to take into it any vibration coming from the Supreme Being (Purusha). It shines in its own splendour. That shining is that enables it to be recognised.

Coming down from the Mahat, we have the next entity in Creation, Ahankara, i.e., the sense of 'I'. The moment Ahankara comes, the three Gunas—Sattva, Rajas and Tamas—begin to manifest themselves. From Ahankara, when it is mixed up with Tamoguna comes the

Sabda-Tanmatra. It is from the Sabda that Sparsa evolves. From Sparsa comes Rupa; From Rupa, Rasa; from Rasa comes finally Gandha. From the same Ahankara as it is affected by the same Tamoguna, we get the first of the primordial elements, viz., Akasa. From this comes Vayu; from Vayu, Tejas; from Tejas comes Apas; and from Apas comes at last Prithvi.

Likewise, from Ahankara, when it is affected by Rajas, comes the ten Indriyas. From Ahankara, when it is affected by Sattva, comes Manas. (When we speak of Manas, we think of its threefold aspects of intelligence, emotion and will.)

Thus we see that the entire universe has come out of Sakti, the projection of Purusha. What about the Jivas themselves? The scriptural view is that the Jiva is the seer of the universe. He is spoken of as the Drashta and the universe is the Drishyam (that which is seen). The Jiva is like Isvara, imperishable—the Amsa or partial manifestation of the Supreme Purusha. This is not the Advaitin's view; but when we are discussing the universe, we are in the region of duality and not of Advaita. The Jivas, therefore, can be spoken of as Amsas or fractions. Each Jiva creates for itself its own mind, its own Indriyas and its own shape, making use of the five Bhutas. That is why each person is different from every other in facial features, mental outlook and spiritual level.

Now it is the Jiva which makes use of its equipment in the form of body, mind and Indriyas for experiencing pain and pleasure and also for finally liberating itself from the contact with the universe. We have seen that the universe itself is only Sakti, variously called as Pradhana, Prakriti or

Alinga. Let us now enquire, in brief, into how this Sakti manifests itself through the different objects in creation.

MANIFESTATION OF SAKTI

We shall start from the mineral kingdom. If we dissolve common salt and copper sulphate in water to the saturation point of each and leave the solution undisturbed for a few days, we shall find that common salt crystals and copper sulphate crystals are deposited in the bottom. Now, who gave the brain to the common salt particles to separate themselves from the copper sulphate particles and from common salt crystals? The answer is that it is the 'mineral Buddhi' (or mind)—the creation of the Jiva embodied in the mineral (common salt or copper sulphate)—that gave the order for the arrangement of the particles in that particular manner. That 'mineral Buddhi' is the universally prevalent Sakti or Prakriti as it manifests itself through the mineral. In the case of the formation of crystals, we have the Sakti showing itself as cohesion. But in the mineral world we have Sakti manifesting itself as heat, light, sound, magnetism and electricity. The highest form in which it shows itself is as electricity. We can call this manifestation of Sakti the name of Bhuta Sakti for the reason that it is revealed by the things made up of the Pancha-Bhutas.

Passing on to the plant world, we notice that the Sakti shows itself in a higher degree. The plant has the power of taking in food through water, etc., and it consequently grows. There we see life or Prana. This Sakti has to be called Prana-Sakti because it is different from electricity. It is not merely proton and electron. We often see big plants—usually banyan plants—growing on the top of temple walls, breaking those stone-walls. The life-energy in the growing plant is greater and more powerful than the electron energy in the stone-wall. That manifestation of the cosmic Sakti through plants may be called Prana-Sakti.

If we now go to the animal world, we shall find that animals have a still higher form of energy. They have got the mind which can find out relations to a certain extent—between cause and effect, and which can have a more acute sense of pain and pleasure. The animal-mind will also show will-power. This is Manas-sakti. It is superior in kind and not merely in degree to the Prana-Sakti of the plant. As against the Manas-sakti of the animal, the Prana-Sakti of the plant is nowhere.

ATMA-SAKTI

Above the ordinary animal stands man. He has not merely discrimination but also the aesthetic and the ethical sense, in other words, he has the full use of the intellectual, emotional and volitional powers. That is why he stands far above the animal. His Sakti may be spoken of as the Jiva-Sakti, because the Jiva embodied in a human being makes full use of the Manas and the Indriyas.

Beyond the ordinary Jiva-Sakti, which every human being has, there is the special Sakti which we find in saints, who are able to have full control of their minds. The great Yogi who is expert in Chitta-Vritti-Nirodha, i.e., the control of the modifications of the mind, has what we may call Atma-Sakti, because when he has cleared the mind of its agitations, it receives the energy of the Atman residing in his body. This is the highest form of Sakti which man, as man, can aspire for.

When the perfect man lays down his body, he is free to remain apart from the Paramatman or to merge himself in it. If he chooses to remain separate, he will be rendering service to the different orders of beings in the universe. In doing so, they will be making use of Chit-Sakti (which is also Atma-Sakti) and thus helping God in the discharge of His functions.

3

MOTHER-WORSHIP

(Dr. T.M.P. Mahadevan)

There is an exquisite verse in the Svetasvatara Upanishad, exquisite both in form and meaning which reads: "Thou art woman; Thou art man; Thou art lad, and the maiden too; Thou art the old man who totters with a stick; Thou art born with Thy face turned everywhere." In myriad forms God appears. In the gracefulness of woman and in the strength of man, in the joy of youth and in the wisdom of age, the Divine Power manifests itself.

This is not all. It is God's Sakti that creates all things, sustains them and withdraws them unto itself. And as Power and the Possessor of Power are non-different, God Himself has often been conceived as She.

The Motherhood of God is a very old conception. Among the relics of ancient civilisation are to be found images of the Mother Goddess. In one of the hymns of the Rig-Veda, Sakti is described as residing in heaven and supporting the earth. In another passage the goddess Aditi (meaning the 'Boundless') is identified with all gods and all men, with 'whatever has been and whatever shall be.' In the Taittiriya Upanishad the teacher, while giving his final instruction to the pupil says: 'Regard thy mother as a god.' In the Kenopanishad a story is told of Indra, the king of the Devas, who, on account of the pride of power and victory, could not recognise God when He appeared before him and had to receive wisdom from the Mother. Then in the same region of the sky, Indra came across a woman who was shining brightly, Uma the daughter of Himavan. He asked Her, 'What Spirit is this?' She replied: 'It is Brahman.' And there are a host of minor Upanishads which speak of Sakti as the highest Being, as the absolute Brahman, one without a second.

MATRILATRY

A system of philosophy and a set of occult practices have been woven round Matrilatry or Mother-worship in India. And Saktism has been one of the potent forces for the spiritual regeneration of the Hindus, though in corrupt times and practised by ineligibles, it has led to certain abuses. The Saktas accept the Vedas as the basic scriptures and the Sakta-Tantras as texts expounding the means to attain the goal set forth in the Vedas. As the Kamika Agama puts it, the Tantra is so called because it explains (Tanoti) in great detail knowledge concerning Tattva (truth) and Mantra (mystic syllables) and because it saves (Tranat). Tantra is the saving knowledge, the craft which carries the soul safely to the port of freedom. It is wrong to regard the Tantras as books of necromancy, magic spells and mysterious formulae. They are open scriptures from which all persons without distinctions of caste, creed or colour may draw inspiration. They are primarily Sadhana-Sastras, the teaching about the paths to perfection.

ADVAITA SAKTISM

The metaphysical position of Advaita or non-dualism is taken over by the Sakta as the foundational theme. Reality is one, and that is Satchidananda, Existence, Consciousness, Bliss. As Sir John Woodroffe points out, "Sakta doctrine is a special presentation of the so-called Monism (Advaita: Lit. 'not-two'), and Sakta ritual, even in those condemned forms which have given rise to the abuses by which this scripture is most generally known, is a practical application of it. The Sakta subscribes without reservation to the view that ultimate Reality is one, of the nature of Pure Consciousness or Experience 'per se and that it is the ground of the manifest universe which appears therein through Maya. But while the Advaita of Sankara would regard this appearance as illusory, the Advaita of the Sakta would consider it to be real. Maya in Saktism is not the indeterminable nescience that somehow illusorily manifests the world, but real power or Sakti identical with ultimate Reality, causing the origination, sustention and destruction of the universe. Pure Consciousness as the unperturbed substrate (Nirguna Brahman) is Siva. The same Reality in the Creative Force or the *'elan vital'* is Sakti." The Sammohana Tantra says: "Without Prakriti or Sakti the transmigratory world cannot be. Without Purusha or Siva true knowledge cannot be attained. Therefore both should be worshipped—the Mahakali and the Mahakala." The Absolute is a word, is Siva-Sakti, Man-Woman, or God-power. It evolves into the world of finite existence, and yet does cease to be what it is, namely, pure Consciousness, Existence and Bliss. The individual soul or the Pasu-Jiva is none other than Siva. Through limitation it feels estranged, or sundered from its moorings. Through sublimation it is resolved, along with the universe, into the unitary Consciousness which is perfect Bliss.

THE TRINITY

Popular religion has identified Sakti with Mahadevi (*magna mater*), the eternal Spouse of Siva and the adorable Sister of Narayana. But the Saktas realise that the Supreme Mother transcends the divine trinity of Brahma, Vishnu and Rudra. She is Durga or Power as Action (Kriya); She is Lakshmi or Power as Will (Iccha); She is Sarasvati or Power as Knowledge (Jnana). For the first three days of Navaratri She is worshipped as Durga, for the second three days as Lakshmi, and for the last three days as Sarasvati. And on the tenth day She is adored as Rajarajesvari, the Queen-Mother transcending the triple aspects that go to constitute the changing world.

CREATION AND DESTRUCTION

A unique feature of Hinduism, in general, and of Saktism, in particular, is that the powers of destruction are not delegated to Satan standing opposite and alien to God. The Mother not only creates but also destroys. Death loses all its horror when it is regarded as a portal to new life. Destruction is no destruction when it leads to a fresh mode of existence. Just as creation is an expression of the divine power, so too is destruction. Hence the Sakta conceives of the Mother both as Tripurasundari, the beautiful creatrix and as the terrific Kali, the dark Goddess, who revels in the dance of death. Swami

Vivekananda captures the spirit of the Sakta in a hymn to Kali where he sings:

> "Come Mother, come!
> For Terror is Thy name,
> Death is in Thy breath,
> And every shaking step
> Destroys a world for ever;
> Thou time, the All-destroyer!
> Come, O Mother, come!"

SYMBOL OF BRAHMAN

It is often criticised that Saktism is 'a doctrine teaching the primacy of the Female and thus fit only for suffragette monists,' that is 'a mere feminisation of orthodox Vedanta.' That this criticism is pointless will be evident when one understands the implications of the Saktas-doctrine. It is no more wrong to call God as Mother than to call Him Father. From the empirical point of view, both the principles, static and dynamic, male and female, are needed for explaining world-creation. The Sakta lays the emphasis on the female because, while the man's part in procreation is fleeting and momentary, the woman's part is more abiding and intimate. The Supreme Mother sacrifices Herself to become the world. And so, from this point of view, the Mother-conception is more important than the Fatherhood of God. At the same time the Sakta knows well that from the transcendental standpoint the distinctions of sex have no application to the Absolute. The Sanskrit word Matri (in English 'Mother') is both feminine and masculine. The Mahakala-Samhita addresses the Mother thus in a hymn: "Thou art neither girl, nor maid, nor old. Indeed, Thou art neither female, nor male, nor neuter. Thou art inconceivable, immeasurable Power, the Being of all which exists, void of all duality, the Supreme Brahman, attainable only through illumination or wisdom."

Om Saktimayam Jagat

4

THE SAKTA SYSTEM

(Sri Dewan Bahadur K.S. Ramaswamy Sastrigal)

The Sakti philosophy also is as old as the Vedas. I do not think that there is any real basis for the Western view which is echoed by Dr. Radhakrishnan when he says: "Sakti Worship, there is no doubt, prevailed originally among the non-Aryans and was gradually adopted by the Aryans." The Rig-Veda refers to Rudrani and Bhavani. The Devi Sukta in the Rig-Veda (X-125) is a real source of the Sakti doctrine. It says: "I am the Sovereign Queen, the treasury of all treasures; the chief of all objects of worship whose all-pervading self all Devatas manifest, whose birth place is in the midst of the causal waters; whose breathing forth gives form to the created worlds and earth extends beyond them, so vast am I in greatness." In it and in Sri Sukta, Bhu Sukta, Neela Sukta and Durga Sukta we have the Central truth of Sakti enunciated in wonderful words. In the Kenopanishad She is described as Uma, Haimavati, Bahu-Sobhamana (Uma, daughter of Himavan and infinitely radiant) and as bestowing Brahma-vidya on god Indra. In the Devi Upanishad and other Sakta Upanishads Her glory is described in detail. Thus Devi is not only the principle of creation, the principle of auspiciousness, the principle of cosmic energy and the principle of austerity (Tapasi Jvalati), but is also the principle of Divine knowledge. She is Jada-Sakti and Chit-Sakti. She is Iccha-Sakti, Jnana-Sakti and Kriya-Sakti. She is not only the Maya-Sakti but also Moksha-Lakshmi. In the Vaishnava-Agamas, Lakshmi is described as mercy and as the means of salvation. But in the Sakta-Agamas, Devi is described as the creator and ruler of the Universe and as the Saguna aspect of Brahman as well.

In the Puranas also, Her glory is sung. In the Itihasas, She is described as having shown grace to Rama and Arjuna. In the Srimad-Bhagavata, She is described as the sister of Krishna. But it is in the Sakta-Agamas and Tantras and in the Devi-Bhagavata that Her glory is most elaborately sung. The Sakta-Agamas are five Subhajagamas, sixty-four Kantagamas and eight Misragamas. I got from a friend of mine a copy of Agastya's Sakti-Sutras which deserve a wide circulation and homage. The famous poems attributed to Sri Sankara viz., Sivanandalahari and Soundaryalahari show how he revelled in the worship and adoration of Siva and Devi. Bhaskararaya's commentary on the Lalita Sahasranama is a valuable work. The enthusiastic labours of Sir John Woodroffe (Arthur Avalon) have made Tantra works available to the modern reader.

In the Sakti doctrine, Siva is the Supreme unchanging eternal consciousness and Sakti is His kinetic power. Siva and Sakti are described as Prakasa and Vimarsa, i.e., glory and power. Siva is Chit and Sakti is Chidrupini, i.e., static and dynamic consciousness. They are really one. Siva becomes the creator of the Universe through the power of Sakti. If Siva is in union with Sakti, He becomes the Lord of the Universe; if not, He cannot even move. Brahma, Vishnu and Rudra perform the functions of creation, preservation and destruction of the Universe in accordance with the will of Sakti. It is from Her that Tirodhana (obscuration of the Divine nature) and Anugraha (grace revelatory of Divine nature) come.

The course of manifestation is Siva, Sakti, Nada, Bindu and Suddhamaya. From Maya which assumes the form of Prakriti comes the evolution of the Universe, the total number of categories being thirty-six as in the Saiva Tantras. The Jivas are Amsas of Siva and are really one with Siva. Sir John Woodroffe says in his Sakti and Sakta: "The function of Prakriti is to veil, limit or finalise pure infinite formless consciousness, so as to produce form, for without such limitation there cannot be the appearance of form." These Gunas work by mutual suppression. The function of Tamas is to veil consciousness, of Sattva to reveal it and of Rajas the active principle to make either Tamas suppress Sattva or Sattva suppress Tamas. The forms of life are therefore the stairs (Sopana) on which man mounts to the state of infinite, eternal and formless bliss.

One peculiar feature is that Siva is described as Satchidananda, Nirvikara (changeless), Nishkala (partless), Nirmala (untouched by Maya), Nirguna (without attributes), Arupa (without form) and all-pervasive like space. Sri John Woodroffe says: "The Sakta Tantra is thus Advaita Vada, for it proclaims that Paramatma and Jivatma are one." One of the Devi's names in Lalita Sahasranama is "Brahmatmaika-svarupini" (whose nature is of the identity of Brahman and Atman). The Sammohana Tantra says in Chapter VIII that Sri Sankaracharya was an incarnation of Lord Siva for the destruction of Buddhism. The Sakti worshipper is asked to meditate at dawn on the following verse:

"I am the Devi and none other. I am Brahman who is beyond all grief. I am of the form of Satchidananda and am eternally free in my nature."

The great glory of the Sakti doctrine is its affirmation that the Universe is Power—a manifestation of Devi's glory. But Power is not blind physical force but is the power of knowledge, the power of bliss, the power of love (Chit-Sakti, Ananda-Sakti, Prema-Sakti). While not denying the Advaita doctrine that from the standpoint of noumenal reality there is in reality no creation at all, the Sakti-Sastras which are Sadhana-Sastras describe the Universe as the manifestation of Sakti.

Another great aspect of the Sakti philosophy is the emphasis placed by it on Yoga by which the higher energies in us can be awakened and brought into play to help the world and to enable us to realise the Supreme. It teaches us how to awaken the Kundalini Sakti and pierce the six centres of power (Shatchakras) and realise the ineffable glory of Siva-Sakti in the Sahasrara (the spiritual centre in the brain).

A third great feature of the doctrine is the emphasis laid by the system on mystic Mantras and worship, though all the Sadhanas, i.e., Nishkama Karma, Bhakti, Yoga and Jnana are accepted as Sadhanas (means of liberation)

It is true in some degraded forms of Saktism that there have been magic and immorality and seeking of occult powers. The theory of the five Makaras—Madya or wine, Mamsa or flesh, Matsya or fish, Mudra or symbolical acts, and Maithuna (sexual union)—is a travesty of the truth. But it is not proper to undermine the pure doctrine on account of its temporary degradations and corruptions. Sir John Woodroffe says well: "Ritual is an art, the art of religion. Art is the outward material expression of ideas intellectually held and emotionally felt. Ritual art is concerned with the expression of these ideas and feelings which are specifically called religious. It is a mode by which religious truth is presented, and made intelligible in material forms and symbols to the mind. It appeals to all natures passionately sensible of that beauty in which, to some, God most manifests Himself. But it is more than this, for it is the means by which the mind is transformed and purified. The Sakta is thus taught that He is one with Siva and His power of Sakti. This is not a matter of mere argument. It is a matter of experience. It is ritual Yoga practice which secures that experience for them."

The concept of the Motherhood of God is a most beautiful, tender and attractive concept. The Gita says: "I am the Father of the Universe. I am the Mother of the Universe." The Sakti cult is open to all, including women. God is neither male nor female. Gender has no place in the concepts of Divinity. But the Mother aspect of God is no less true than the Father aspect and is infinite mercy, love and grace.

Om Saktimayam Jagat

5

SAKTI

(Sri Yogi Gauri Prasad)

Every year in the latter half of the month of Ashwin (September-October), Hindus, all over Bharatavarsha worship Sri Durga-Devi for nine days continuously, setting up on each of those days a particular image of that Maha-Sakti Devi, and conclude that worship on the 10th day or the Vijayadasami Day.

Let us consider: what does all this signify and how does this religious worship help us in fulfilling the aim of human life on this earth-plane. In the Hindu mythology Maha Devi or Mahesvari is considered as the Supreme Sakti or Power of the Supreme Being and is known as Jagadamba, the creatrix of the universe.

According to Sankhya, She is the Mula-Prakriti or Supreme Prakriti of the Supreme Purusha.

The word 'Sakti' comes from the root `Sak' which means 'to be able', 'to do' and this indicates both *activity* and *capacity* therefor. Sakti, because it is the productive or creative principle, is symbolically female, but it is in reality neither male nor female, but only a power which manifests itself in various forms.

Sakti in its static state is Chit-Sakti and in its kinetic state it is Maya-Sakti. (1) As Chit-Sakti She is the Ultimate Changeless Reality and (2) as Maya-Sakti She evolves into and appears in the form of the world. These two are in their essence: (1) the Enduring Real that is Herself and (2) forms of Herself, the passing yet real objects of Experience. According to Sakta-Darshan, the Universe is the product of these two Saktis—Chit-Sakti and Maya-Sakti. It is in the nature of this Ultimate Reality (Chit) to manifest itself. In Chit or Consciousness there is the seed of Power to manifest itself as object to limited centres of it. That seed is the collectivity of all tendencies (Samskaras) towards life and form acquired in an infinite number of past universes. The distinctive changes in such collective tendencies in terms of Time is designated as

Yuga and is classified in accordance with the predominating element of Guna in that collective tendencies. That in which Pure Sattva Guna prevails is called Satya-Yuga and so on.

We thus see that Sakti means both power in general and every particular form of power. Life is a power of consciousness or Chitta. Mind also is a power and so is matter. Mind is constantly functioning in the form of Vrittis. Reasoning, will and feeling or Bhava and so forth are all aspects of mind-power in its general sense. Power translated to the material plane is force and therefore only one and the grossest aspect of Sakti or Power.

In short, all these aspects or special powers are limited forms of the Great Creative Power, the Mata Durga-Devi, the Mother (Ambika) of the Universe. It is She who personalises in the form of all beings in the universe; and it is She again who, as the essence of such personalisations, is the Supreme Personality who in manifestation is 'God in action.' Worship of Maha-Sakti is not, therefore, worship of these limited forms, but of the Divine Will, Knowledge and Action as revealed in the Universe. Worship of mere force is Asuric. Force, however, may be moralised by the good purpose which it serves. The antithesis is not rightly between might and right, but between might in the service of the right and might in the service of the wrong. To worship force merely is to worship matter.

SIMILARITY BETWEEN SANKHYA SYSTEM AND SAKTA DOCTRINE OF SAKTI

It has been stated above that in terms of Sankhya system, Maha-Sakti is the Mula-Prakriti of the Supreme Purusha. Speaking in a general way, we may convert the second element of that system, viz., the Infinite Purushas into one Siva and Prakriti into Siva's Power or Sakti and then affirm that Siva and Sakti are not as the Sankhya says two independent Realities, but one Reality in twin aspect—static and kinetic—and thus perceive some similarity between the Sankhya and the Sakta doctrines of Sakti. Sankhya Purusha is changeless Consciousness (Chit). So is Siva. Prakriti is, as unlimited cause, the principle of change, and as effect, limited changing forms, which are as effects or modifications of their cause. Similarly, Sakti is that which in itself unchangeable, produces forms out of itself, as material cause, the world of change. In common language, we speak of the Power or Sakti of Siva, but strictly Sakti is Siva; there is no Siva without Sakti nor Sakti without Siva. This substantial unity with diversity of aspects involves another distinct view of the nature of cosmic process. In Sankhya there are two realities; in Sakti-doctrine there is only one with dual aspect.

As we are dealing here with the Power-aspect of Consciousness to recollect and imagine forth the universe, we may speak only of Power or Sakti, if we are careful to remember that the universe is the product of Chit-Sakti and Maya-Sakti, that is, Chit or Consciousness in its aspect as power and efficient cause and Maya-Sakti or power as material cause. There is thus one ultimate enduring absolute Reality of which all other relative realities as mind, life and matter are transient forms.

The Ultimate Reality is Eternal Being-Consciousness (Sat-Chit) which in itself is changeless. Consciousness whether transcendent or immanent never changes nor moves. If in the world-process it appears to do so, this is due to the modes of mind of which it is the basis. But this consciousness is nevertheless a true efficient cause, that is, one which moves without itself being moved. As such, it is consciousness-power (Chit-Sakti). But it may be asked what is this Substance-Energy which is the material cause of this universe?

The answer depends on how we look at it. If we look at it from the other-world aspect, that is, the Reality which we call Sakti or Power as it is in itself, then the answer is that it is consciousness (Chidrupini Sakti). If we look at it on this-world side, then it is the Root-Substance-Energy of the Universe which appears as mind and matter. That root as cause is however neither the one nor the other, but the Power (Maya-Sakti) to produce to itself and to appear as both, when consciousness becomes outward-turned (Bahirmukhi) and sees in its gradual awakening to the world, the 'This' (Idam) or Universe.

THE TWO ATTITUDES OR
STATES OF CONSCIOUSNESS

Consciousness has two attitudes, inner (Antarmukhi) and outward-turned (Bahirmukhi). In the first and in its fullest sense, there is an experience in which there is no subject or object. In the second, the object or 'This' (Idam) is gradually experienced at first as part of and then outside itself. There is a polarisation in the (first) unitary consciousness of 'I' (Aham) and 'This' (Idam), the experiencing subject and his world. The latter is as real as the former which perceives it, but since both are transient and change their reality is relative. Full, timeless, spaceless, endless, persistence is the Absolute Real which is the Supreme Experience. In the Sakta-Sastras the evolution of consciousness in 36 Tattvas or stages into mind and matter has been explained in great detail and complication and in technical terms of their own. They show the origin of even Purusha and Prakriti. In fact Purusha and Prakriti Tattvas merely mark the stage of evolution or vibration, when the 'This' (Idam) or object of the 'I' (Aham) is thrown out of the Self and becomes an outer thing distinct from it. In other words, they (Purusha and Prakriti) are the immediate root of empirical reality, but that root is itself grounded in the soil of consciousness which is ultimately Samvit or the Supreme (Chidrupini) Experience Itself. This is Maya-Sakti to the Sakta. She in one aspect is the ultimate changeless Reality. She in another aspect does evolve into and appear in the forms of the world.

There is thus a real yet transient diversity in a real and enduring unity. Doubtless this doctrine does not explain how logically Goddess (Sakti-Devi) can be changeless and yet change. But in this respect the Maya of Sankaracharya which is neither real nor unreal also runs counter to logic. The highest truth is alogical. The Sakta says, "better accept both the reality of the changing world which is imposed by Maya on us in our ordinary experience, as also the reality of the changeless which is experienced in Yoga." In spiritual experience the problem disappears. And, so Siva says in the Kularnava Tantra: "Some desire dualism (Dvaitavada), others monism (Advaitavada). Such, however, know not My truth which is beyond both monism and dualism (Dvaitadvaitavivarjita)." The Sakta-Tantras are a form of Advaita-Vedanta. All worshippers are practical realists whatever their doctrine may be. A Sakta prays to the Mother (Durga-Devi) knowing that the form of the One as Mother is that in which

---

She appears to him. This feature of the Sakta doctrine is well illustrated in the Devi-Bhagavatam. The narration runs thus:

When Siva refused His wife Sati-Devi permission to attend the Yajna of Her father Daksha, even though She repeatedly besought it, the Jagadamba-Devi seeing that Her husband's vanity had influenced Him, assumed a very terrible form with the object of shattering that vanity. Pondering for a moment in Her mind, Sati opened Her three fearful eyes and overpowered Sankara (Siva) with illusion. Siva stood still looking at the Devi, with Her lips parted in anger and eyes shining like destructive fire. On being thus looked at, the Devi suddenly displayed the terrible teeth in Her terrible mouth and laughed aloud. On hearing that frightful sound of laughter Sankara Mahadeva was paralysed with fright. Opening His three eyes with great effort, Siva saw (but once) the world-terrifying aspect of Jagadamba. When He looked upon Her, Her body immediately lost its golden colour and took on that of a dark mass of crushed eye-paint (Anjana). She appeared naked as space, with dishevelled hair, with a lolling tongue and four arms. She was terribly furious, bathed in sweat (caused by Her anger) and of frightful countenance, garlanded with skulls, bearing on Her head the brilliant crown and a crescent moon, shining like 10 million suns. Her voice thundered loudly. In such a fearful aspect Sati stood dazzling by the mass of Her own brilliant Tejas (energy) before Mahadeva and uttered loud peals of laughter. Seeing that wonderful appearance of the Devi, Sankara lost all self-control and in panic sought to flee in all directions. Seeing Siva thus overcome with fear, the Devi again uttered peal after peal of dreadful laughter and with the object of reassuring Him shouted "Fear not! Fear not!" Hearing this cry and fierce peal of laughter Mahadeva frantically rushed again in flight in every direction. But in whatever direction He ran He saw a fearful form before Him. After having thus run towards each of the ten quarters of the heaven, He saw none without danger for Him; so He sat down on earth and shut His three eyes and when He opened them He saw before Him Syama (black lady) with a smiling face, Her eyes wide and terrible and Her hair dishevelled. Seeing Her thus, Mahadeva, as if in great fear asked, "Who art Thou, Syama? Where has My beloved wife Sati gone?"

Devi said: "Mahadeva, I am Thy Sati here standing before Thee. Why is Thy mind so confused today? Do I appear to Thee different from Thy Sati?"

Siva said: "If Thou really art My beloved Sati (daughter of Daksha) why has Thou become black and fearful? Who are these forms of terrible shape, standing in all directions around Me? Amongst these which art Thou? Tell Me everything for these wonderful forms have made Me greatly afraid."

Sati said: "I am the subtle (beyond the reach of speech and mind) Mulaprakriti who creates and destroys. Owing to the promise I had aforetime given to Thee (to bless Thee for Thy Tapasya) I incarnated as a fair girl in Daksha's house merely to get and charm Thee as My husband. I have today assumed this fearful aspect to terrify Daksha alone. The ten terrible forms which Thou seest in each of the ten directions are each of them My aspects. Seeing Thee so greatly afraid and turning in all directions I stood before Thee blocking them by these, the forms of Mine.

Siva said: "Thou art the subtle Mulaprakriti who creates, preserves and destroys. It is not possible that one should know Thee who art beyond the reach of speech and mind. So, not knowing Thee, through great illusion, I have said unpleasant words to Thee. Pardon Me, O Paramesvari, the offence I have thus committed. Tell Me the names of each of these ten dreadful forms of Thine, standing in each of the ten quarters."

Devi said: "The dark-coloured form with terrible eyes which Thou does see before Thee is Kali. She who is above Thee of Syama (dark blue) colour is Mahamaya Tara, the very image of Mahakali. The lean destitute and very frightful Devi whom Thou seest on Thy right side is, O high-souled Mahadeva, Mahavidya Chinnamasta. O Sambhu, the Devi on Thy left side is Bhuvanesvari. She who is behind You is Devi Bagalamukhi, destroyer of foes. She who appears as a widow on the south-east is Devi Mahavidya Dhumavati, great Isvari. The Devi on the south-west is Tripurasundari (Kamala). In the north-west is Matangi and in the north-east Mahavidya Shodasi, a great Isvari. She who is below You is Bhairavi. O Sambhu! Be not afraid. Of My many forms (90 millions of manifestations) these ten are the best (the most perfect Vibhutis)." (Vibhuti is the thing which characterises the higher nature. Vibhu is one who is all-pervading and Vibhuti is both that which it displays and the power by which it displays.)

From the above Puranic story we thus gather that the ten Devis are the ten principal Divine Saktis meant to overcome and resist all Asuric elements in this world which pervade in all the ten dimensions of this globe.

All this is not a figure of speech or an imaginary symbol; but sublime conscious bodies of power and energy that emanate and come down from the supreme abode to uplift the earth-consciousness and divinise it in the human beings. These deities are Names, Powers and Personalities of the Universal Godhead and they represent each some essential might and energy of the Supreme Divine Being. They manifest the cosmos and are manifest in it. They recognise in the soul of man their brother and ally and desire to help and increase him by themselves increasing in him, so as to possess his world with their Light, Strength and Beauty. These deities call man to a divine companionship and alliance; they attract and uplift him to their fraternity, invite his aid and offer theirs against the sons of darkness and division—the Asuric element in man.

Man in return calls the deities to his sacrifice, offers to them his own mind, power and will, and receives them back re-enlightened, re-inforced and re-strengthened as their gifts into his being and into his life. Gods or their Saktis as Goddesses are not simply poetical personifications of abstract ideas or of psychological and physical functions of Nature. To the Vedic seers they were living realities; the vicissitude of the human soul represents a cosmic struggle not merely of principles and tendencies, but of the Cosmic Powers which support and embody them. These are the Devatas and demons or Asuras. On the world-stage and in the individual soul the same real drama and play with the same personages is enacted.

What is the purpose of this Play; what is the end to be achieved? It is, of course, coming down of the Supreme

Chit-Sakti or Power-Consciousness to the physical or material consciousness and establishing itself as the supreme all-ruling element in the human being. It is only then that it takes direct charge of the work to be done in and through the human system. But, before the arrival of the hour of that coming down, much work has to be done for preparing the human instrument by its own Yoga-force which is a special Power of the Supreme Being, a subtle instrument for the purification of the being and making it fit to receive and hold the infiltrations of the forces of strength and knowledge and peace into the system.

Now let us carefully study and make a brief note of some of these cardinal principles of this system of what is commonly expressed as 'The Tantra' or 'The Tantra Sastra.' The use of this expression itself is due to a misconception and leads to others. The word 'Tantra' has been derived from the root 'Tan' to spread. Tantra is that (Sastra or scripture) by which knowledge is spread. The suffix 'Tra' is from the root 'to save.' That knowledge is spread which saves (*Tanyate vistaryate jnanam anena iti tantram*). What is that but religious knowledge which saves? So, Tantra Sastra is a treatise which deals with that Knowledge. Knowledge in the Sastric sense is actual immediate (Sakshatkara) experience or demonstration, not mere reading about it in books, however divine and however useful as a preliminary such study may be. Tantras were thus regarded rather as a scientific discovery than as a revelation; that is something discovered by the self rather than from without. Tantras are thus claimed to be the revealed means by which the Tattvas and other matters and powers may be discovered. In short, the Tantra Sastras or Agamas form a practical philosophy, i.e., a philosophy which not merely argues but experiments. In fact, all must act who have not achieved. For this reason every ancient faith has its ritual.

A Western writer has expressed the opinion that the Tantra Sastra was at least in its origin alien and indeed hostile to the Vedas. He said that "We are strongly of the opinion that in their essence, the two principles are fundamentally opposed and that the Tantras only used Vedic forms to mask its essential opposition." This is not a correct view to take. Ignorant notions prevail on the subject of the relation of the Tantras to Vedas and the Vedas to Tantras. From an outside standpoint the historical speculation is that the worship of the Great Mother, the *magna mater* of the Near East, the Adya Sakti of the Sakta Tantra in its essentials is one of the oldest and most widespread religions in the world, and one which in India was possibly, in its origin independent of the Brahmanic religion as presented to us in the Vedic Samhitas and Brahmanas. If this be so, it was later on mingled with the Vedanta tradition, so that the Sakta faith of today is a particular presentation of the general Vedantic teaching. Whatever be the origins of the Sakta doctrines, it would be a mistake to overlook the possibility of the so-called `Tantric' tradition having been fed by ways of thought and practice which were not, in the strict sense of the term, part of the Vaidic cult or in the line of its descent.

The latest tendency in modern Western philosophy is to test upon intuition or superconsciousness, as it was formerly the tendency to glorify dialectics. But intuition, however, has to be led into higher and higher possibilities by means of Sadhana, which is merely the gradual unfolding of the Spirit's vast latent magazine of power or Sakti which everybody possesses in himself. It will be found in the compilation called 'Yati-Dharma-Nirnaya' that even Dandins of Sri Sankara's School follow a Tantric ritual suited to their state.

CONSCIOUSNESS EXPLAINED

Let us, after this digression, revert to our study and dwell on the first principles which form the sheet-anchor of this study of Sakta Sastra. It is a Vedantic dictum that consciousness—Chit—is fundamental to being, to all existence—Sat. It has been axiomatic truth with the mystics and sages of the Upanishads. It is necessary to bear in mind what is meant by consciousness. Obviously it is something aware of itself; it is in man, a self-evident awareness which though subjective, yet is not limited to his subjective being. This is because, although it is infinite and one, still there is in it an inherent power which is immense and deployed in multiple forms of consciousness. We may call it manifestation of the many from the One, Diversity in Unity. In our own psychology we can perceive this twofold distinction in consciousness. One aspect of it is the apprehending consciousness which consists in the awareness 'I am,' the consciousness of I-ness; and another is the comprehending consciousness that 'all is.' Thus, the essential one, the unity of all existence is the basic consciousness on which is founded the manifold development of itself.

The diverse forms it assumes are worked out by the power (Sakti) that is ever implicit in the comprehending movement of the Force in the infinitude of the Supreme Being.

This diversity of forms in the manifestation is released in degrees and kind, in quality and bulk, so much so that we find apparent absence of sentience in matter—what we call inanimate objects. But everywhere consciousness is present; only its manifestation differs in range because the instruments of expression differ in form and quality and kind.

Another point of utmost importance to be noted is that once we accept that consciousness (Chit-Sakti) is omnipresent and infinite, we have also accepted that it is not confined to the boundaries of the three-dimensional space. Apart from its reserve as the unmanifest (Avyakta), it comprehends in its infinitude an essential extension in which it pours out of its inherent force vast masses of energy that go to build the world. This extension is in its root an expansive mood and aspect of the Divine Spirit and should not be confounded with the physical space in which we perceive this stellar universe. We have to bear this fact in mind when we are instructed that creation proceeds from above. It is a statement of the mystics all the world over. In India we find it repeatedly mentioned in the Vedas. In the Vedic text, it is used in the sense of 'The Residual above' (Ucchishta). Obviously it is so termed because any number of creations cannot diminish the infinitude of the Supreme Being that for ever remains above the creation which descends from it. When the Supreme Chit-Sakti of the Supreme Being above deploys certain energies for the creation of the worlds, He remains still inexhaustible and rests there forming the foundation above—Upari-Badhva—for the creation in its downward course. For, while there is no question of direction in regard to the Infinite Consciousness in itself, as there is nothing inside or outside of it, every manifestation in it, thrown into creation out of it has a boundary, which means that it is endowed with the property of direction as related to similar objects of creation as well as to the source and support of its own being in the All-Existence. But this source and foundation of created existence is constantly above the perceiving consciousness in the embodied being, whether the embodiment is individual or universal and cosmic in formation. Nor can we say that there is nothing permanently above the embodied being in spatial terms of the experiencing consciousness on the ground that the perception is purely objective. For it must be noted that all perceptions are subjective and all knowledge of the objective is subjective, nay all the objective existence itself is a manifestation worked out by the Sakti force emanating from the Infinite Consciousness and abides in it; and in this sense the objective existence itself rests in the subjective and apprehending aspect of the consciousness in the unalterable infinitude of the Supreme Being. In this context we must remember that creation starts initially from other dimensions of space (Chidakasa) in the higher altitude of Being, proceeds through various grades in the descending order before arriving at a state in which we perceive its material aspect in physical space.

The cosmos of which our earth is a part occupying the lowest rung—lowest rung because there are many levels above and at the summit is the Godhead, the creative spirit who supports the cosmic system from above and there is the foundation of this created existence. These grades in cosmic existence are really various levels and states of consciousness with their corresponding fields for active participation in the cosmic scheme which we call the planets of being. The cosmic system itself is an embodiment of the divine spirit, the creative Godhead or Isvara presiding over it above and entering into it in a supporting erect column with the higher end at the summit and the lower end here on our earth-plane. This vertical column of support is termed 'Stambha.' In the Atharva Veda (Book X) there are two hymns in which the Godhead has been described as Skamba, the source, support and substance of all that exists. It is the Skamba that upholds (Dadhara). it is the Skamba that enters into and possesses all this universe (Idam Visvam Bhuvanam Avivesha), says the Veda. The Skamba is the cosmic pillar, the spinal column of the cosmic Being, represented in the evolution of the human body, by the backbone, the axial pole or spinal cord, which gives to the human body, its erect posture.

Next we have to remember that in the higher regions of consciousness we do not speak of vehicles, for their place is taken by radiances; the consciousness which has localisation in the physical body, in higher stages of its development, gets concentrated in a centre as a Light-Power from which rays issue forth in all directions. In all crucial stages of evolution when a higher principle is to be evolved, however intense may be the evolutionary urge in the Earth-Spirit, whatever intrinsic merit the evolutionary force may have, the higher principle that waits for manifestation has to await the coming down of a Power from the plenary home of that principle and to lift it up from its submerged wakefulness. This is how life or Chaitanya-Sakti has entered into matter and mind and changed them into living matter for the expression of Spirit through thinking—self-conscious life. This principle technically called Supermind is a Light, which connotes much more than what it literally denotes. It is not a figure of speech or an imaginary symbol, but a sublime conscious body of Light that emanates and comes down from the supreme plane of consciousness (Chit-Sakti) to uplift the earth-consciousness and divinise it in the human being by establishing itself as the supreme principle of all knowledge, life and action in man. It is a special divine power because it is not a Sakti or power generated by human effort in the course of the well-known lines of Sadhana. This Power or Sakti is active in its own right, though the human instrument can and in fact has to contribute to its effectiveness, by submitting to its work, by making an exclusive call upon it, by an all-round willing consent to its working. It is the Daivam (Providence) of the Gita. The wise all-seeing will that is at work in the world (Gita Ch. XVIII, 5, 14).

The Divine Truth, Satyam, as the Vedic Rishis saw, is not a mere static Reality of the metaphysician, but it is ever active by constantly radiating its Chit-Sakti (Will-Power) to feed and sustain the worlds. It has its own way and works in its own right—Ritam. If Satyam is the Truth, the way of working that Truth is Ritam, Right. Hence the triple formula of the Atharva Veda—Satyam, Ritam, Brihat. It is the way of the working of the Truth, that is the Right, the Law which in a later language was denoted by Dharma. It is the way of the Divine illumined Will works, that is the Right, the true Law. The Rishis pray for a knowledge of the Law of Truth—Satya-Dharmaya. It was the Truth-Law which all sages and seers of the Vedic period sought to know and work upon. In fact the two concepts which have played a dominant part in the personal and social life of the people of Bharatavarsha, since the Vedic times are the Satyam and the Ritam. The early seers of Dharma saw that the Truth-Law is really the Truth-Will of the Divine and can operate in life as an inner and spiritual law, as well as a rule of personal conduct. They applied the principle of Dharma—the Sakshat-Krita-Dharmanah—as the way of the Divine Will to all life, personal and public and extended the same to the government of the group-life represented by the State, Rajya Dharma. Thus Dharma became a ruling principle of all life, whose nature is really hidden in the secret-heart, Hridaya. This was the idea of Dharma that the ancients had when they called upon man to look for it within and enjoined that the assent of the heart was necessary to a particular course of action. Even Manu, when he was codifying the laws of ethical conduct used the phrase 'Hridaya-Abhyanujnana.' The true Dharma is the Law of Truth—Satya-Dharma; it is the way that the Divine Will works in each. Mahatma Gandhi applied that Satya-Dharma or Satyagraha to achieve freedom to this country and did it successfully. Therefore, if one wants to be a true doer of divine works, his first aim must be to get rid totally of all personal desires and self-regarding ego. He must grow in the divine consciousness of the Divine Sakti of Satyam, till there is no difference between his own will and the Will of the Divine Mother Sakti. He must regard his life as given to him only for the divine work and to help in the divine manifestation. No motive except the Divine Mother's impulsion in you, no action that is not Her conscious Action in you and through you. There must be no demand for fruit and no seeking for reward; the only fruit for you is the pleasure of the Divine Mother and the fulfilment of Her work, your only reward is a constant progression in Divine Consciousness. While this transformation is being done, it is more than ever necessary to keep oneself free from all taint of the perversion of the Ego. There must be no attachment to the work or the result, no claim to possess the Sakti that should possess you, no pride of the instrument, no vanity or arrogance. When one is completely identified with the Divine Mother Sakti and feels no longer another and separate being, instrument, servant or worker, but truly a child and eternal portion of Her consciousness and force, then perfection will come. He will then know, see and feel that he is a being and power formed by Her out of Herself, put out for Her play, but always safe in Her. The Mother is the Consciousness-Force of the Supreme and far above all She creates. There are three ways of being of the Mother of which we can become aware when we enter into touch of oneness with the Consciousness-Force, that upholds us and the universe, viz., (1) Transcendent, (2) Universal and (3) Individual. As the one transcendent original Sakti, the Mother stands above all the worlds and bears the Supreme Divine in Her eternal consciousness. All is She, for all are parcel and portion of the Divine Consciousness-Force. Nothing can be here or elsewhere but what She decides and the Supreme sanctions; nothing can take shape except what She moved by the Supreme perceives and forms after casting it into seed in Her creating Ananda. The Matri-Sakti, the Universal Mother, works out whatever is transmitted by Her transcendent consciousness from the Supreme and enters into the worlds that She has made; Her presence fills and supports them with the divine spirit and the divine all-sustaining force and delight without which they could not exist. Each is something that She has seen in Her vision, gathered into Her heart of beauty and power, and created in Her Ananda. Nearer to us are the worlds of perfect supramental creation in which the Mother is the supramental Maha-Sakti, a Power of Divine Omniscient Will and Omnipotent Knowledge (Jnana) always apparent in its unfailing works and spontaneously perfect in every process. There all movements are the steps of Truth; there all beings are souls and powers and bodies of the Divine Light; there all experiences are seas, floods and waves of an absolute intense Ananda.

But, here, where we dwell are the worlds of ignorance, of mind and life and body separated in consciousness from their source, of which this earth is a significant centre and its evolution a crucial process. This, too, with all its obscurity and struggle and imperfection is upheld by the Universal Mother; this, too, is impelled and guided to its secret aim by the Maha-Sakti. These powers and personalities are the many divine forms and personalities in which men have worshipped Her under different names throughout the ages. All the scenes of the earth-play have been like a drama arranged, planned and staged by Her with the cosmic Gods for Her assistance and Herself as a veiled actor. In Her deep great love for Her children, She has consented to put on Herself the cloak of this obscurity, condescended to bear the attacks and torturing influences of the powers of the Darkness and the Falsehood, borne to pass through the portals of the birth that is death, taken upon Herself the pangs and sorrows and sufferings of the creation, since it seemed that thus alone could it be lifted to the Light and Joy and

Truth and Eternal Life. This is the great sacrifice called sometimes the sacrifice of the Purusha, but much more deeply the holocaust of Prakriti, the sacrifice of the Divine Mother.

Four great Aspects (Svarupa) of the Divine Mother, four of Her leading Powers and Personalities have stood prominent in Her guidance of this Universe and in Her dealings with this terrestrial play or Lila. To those four great aspects of Saktis we give four great names (1) Mahesvari, (2) Mahalakshmi, (3) Mahasarasvati and (4) Mahakali.

Mahesvari is Her personality of calm witness and comprehending wisdom and tranquil benignity and inexhaustible compassion and sovereign and surpassing majesty and all ruling greatness. She is the mighty and wise One who opens us to the supramental infinities and the cosmic vastness, to the grandeur of the Supreme Light, to a treasure-house of all Divine Knowledge, to the measureless movement of the Divine Mother's movement. To the wise She gives a greater and more luminous wisdom; those that have vision She admits to Her counsels. Though She is above all, bound by nothing, attached to nothing in the universe, yet She has more than any other the heart of the Universal Mother.

Mahalakshmi is vivid and sweet and wonderful with Her deep aspect of beauty and harmony and fine rhythm, Her intricate and subtle opulence, Her compelling attraction and captivating grace. Where there is affinity to the rhythm of the secret world-bliss (Ananda) and response to the call of the all-beautiful and concord, unity and the glad flow of many lives turned towards the Divine, in that atmosphere She consents to abide. But all that is ugly and base, all that is poor, sordid and squalid, all that is brutal and coarse repels Her advent. Where She finds Herself in man's heart surrounded with selfishness and hatred and jealousy and malignance and envy and strife, a divine disgust seizes upon Her and She withdraws. Even ascetic bareness and harshness are not pleasing to Her, nor the suppression of the heart's deeper emotions and the rigid repression of the soul's and life's part of beauty. For it is through love and beauty that She lays on men the yoke of the Divine. Admitted to the heart, She reveals to it the mystic secrets of the ecstasy that surpasses all knowledge, meets devotion with the passionate attraction of the Divine and lifts wisdom to the pinnacles of wonder and casts on perfection the charm that makes it endure for ever.

Mahasarasvati is the Mother's power of work and Her spirit of perfection and order. She is the most skilful in executive faculty and the nearest to physical Nature while Mahesvari lays down the large lines of the world-forces, Mahakali drives their energy and impetus, Mahalakshmi discovers their rhythms and measures; but Mahasarasvati presides over their detail of organisation and execution, relation of parts and effective combination of forces and unfailing exactitude of result and fulfilment. The science and craft and technique of things are Mahasarasvati's province. Nothing short of a perfect perfection satisfies Her and She is ready to face an eternity of toil if that is needed for the fullness of Her creation. Therefore of all the Mother's power She is the most long-suffering with man and his thousand imperfections. A mother to our wants, a friend in our difficulties, a persistent and tranquil counsellor and mentor, chasing away with Her radiant smile the clouds of gloom and fretfulness and depression; She is firm, quiet and persevering in the deep and continuous urge that drives us towards the integrality of the higher nature. All the work of the other powers leans on Her for its completeness.

Mahakali is of another nature. Not wideness but height, not wisdom but force and strength are Her peculiar powers. There is Her an overwhelming intensity, a mighty passion of force to achieve, a divine violence rushing to shatter every limit and obstacle. Terrible is Her face to the Asura, dangerous and ruthless Her mood against the haters of the Divine; for She is the warrior of the worlds who never shrinks from the battle. Indifference, negligence and sloth in the divine work She cannot bear and She smites awake at once with sharp pain, if need be, the untimely slumberer and loiterer. She, too, is the Mother and Her love is as intense as Her wrath; and She has a deep and passionate kindness. If Her anger is dreadful to the hostile and the vehemence of Her presence painful to the weak and timid, She is loved and worshipped by the great, the strong and the noble, for they feel that Her blows beat what is rebellious in their material into strength and perfect truth, hammer straight what is wry and perverse and expel what is impure and defective. Nothing can satisfy Her that falls short of the supreme ecstasies, the highest heights, the noblest aims, the largest vistas. Therefore, with Her is the victorious force of the divine, and it is by grace of Her fire and passion and speed if the great achievement of life can be done now rather than hereafter.

Mahesvari or Mahamaya is the Supreme Power. In Tantric Sastra the power-holder and the power are as such one, though the transformations of power are many. We speak of transformation or evolution because power and its holder are held to be both the efficient and material cause of the world. Strictly speaking creation (*ex nihilo*) is not taught by any system of Hinduism. But each system presupposes some 'potential matter' out of which the world is evolved in recurring cycles from eternity to eternity. By 'potencial matter' in this statement is meant that which in itself is not matter prime or otherwise, but is the cause of the becoming, amongst other things of the material world. That cause is the power of consciousness which in Tantric is known as 'Maya-Sakti.' This Cosmic Power, though itself unmeasured and undefined, measures out (the root meaning of the word Maya) or makes finite forms in the formless Infinite, which together (form and formless) constitute one alogical Whole (Purna). This Power was called the *magna mater* in the antique West and in India is named Maya when it finitises; and Maha-Maya when it liberates from the finite. The ground of man's being is the Supreme 'I' (Purusha), which though in Itself beyond finite personality, is yet ever finitely personalising as the beings of the Universe. 'Sa-aham' (She I am): this is the Supreme Maya-Sakti, known in Tantra Sastra as Mahesvari.

Until there is in fact a change, Maya-Sakti is merely the potency of becoming in Being and as such is wholly one with the Mother Sakti. But Potency or Power as the material cause contains its effect and the latter is the cause modified. That Cause is the Power of Consciousness, which as the individual centre divides itself into Self and not-Self, as the Consciousness-Whole.

Creation is movement, an uncoiling of Maya-Sakti. Hence the world is called 'Jagat' in Sanskrit which means 'what moves.' As the nature of this movement is circular or spiral the world is said to have evolved in recurring cycles.

This Chit-Sakti, when it manifests as energy, i.e., Maya-Sakti, has a twin-aspect of potencial and kinetic energy.

That power of Chit from which form is derivable, i.e., the power which produces form is called Prakriti-Sakti. This Prakriti-Sakti is the immediate source and the constituent of mind and matter. The corresponding conscious (Chit) aspect of the same Power is Purusha. Prakriti is the kinetic and Purusha, the static aspect of Maya-Sakti.

We thus get the scientific doctrine that to every form of activity there is a static background, negation being a function of Sakti. For instance, just as an atom or electron consists of a static centre around which moving forces revolve, so in the human body Kundalini is the earth-centre—the static centre (Kendra) round which Prana-Sakti in its kinetic aspect as the forces of the body, work. The whole body as the vehicle of mind and matter (as Sakti of the Tattvas) is in ceaseless movement; and the Kundalini (static) Sakti is the immobile support of all these movements. In this connection we have to remember that there is no vehicle of mind and matter which does not display in varying degree some Chit-Sakti or Consciousness and there is no vehicle of Consciousness which is not in perpetual motion. In the universe Mahesvari is the Static Aspect of the

Maha-Maya-Sakti and Maha-Kali, Maha-Lakshmi and Maha-Sarasvati, the various Cosmic, Kinetic Saktis ever working in this globe of our earth-plane. Cosmic creative evolution being in the nature of a polarisation in being into Static and Kinetic aspects of Chit-Sakti thus differs from evolution in the universe itself.

While in the creative evolution of the universe, from the standpoint of Chit-Sakti, it is true that the Cosmic Being or Isvara is the cause of the universe, yet it is also equally true that while the universe as effect is the cause modified, the Cause as cause remains what it was, is and will be, e.g., light from light.

But in the case of evolution in the universe itself, the material cause when producing an effect ceases to be what it was, e.g., milk turned into curd ceases to be milk. We have to bear this basic distinction always in mind when dealing with creative Sakti of Para-Brahman as Creator of the Universe and evolution in the created universe itself.

According to Sakta doctrine, the universe is a Dynamism—an expression of Sakti (kinetic) and an infinite reservoir of Power or Sakti (Static). It is, however, auto-dynamic as such expression of Power or Sakti.

From the Vedantic or metaphysical point of view, Pure Chit-Sakti as Supreme Will is the efficient cause (Nimitta) and Maya-Sakti as Mula-Prakriti is the instrumental and material (Upadana) cause of the Universe. Metaphysically speaking, it may be said that the whole creation is a movement between two involutions, spirit in which all is involved and out of which all evolves downward to the other pole of matter, and matter in which also all is involved and out of which all evolves upward to the other pole of Spirit.

There are other great personalities of the Divine Mother, but they are more difficult to bring down and have not stood out in front with as much prominence in the evolution of the earth-spirit. There are among them Presences indispensable for the supramental realisation—most of all one who is Her Personality of what mysterious and powerful ecstasy and Ananda which flows from a supreme divine Love, the Ananda that holds the key of a wonderful divinest life and even now supports from its secrecies the work of all the other Powers of the Universe. But, human nature, bounded, egoistic and obscure, is inapt to receive these great Presences or to support their mighty action. Only when these Four have founded their harmony and freedom of movement in the transformed mind, life and body, can those other rare Powers manifest in the earth-movement and the supramental action become possible. If you desire this transformation, put yourself in the hands of Mother and Her Powers without cavil or resistance and let Her do unhindered Her work within you.

Three things you must have—consciousness, plasticity and unreserved surrender. For you must be conscious in your mind, soul, heart, life and the very cells of your body, aware of the Mother and Her Power and their working; for although She can and does work in you even in your obscurity and your unconscious parts and moments, it is not the same thing as when you are in an awakened and living communion with Her. The unreserved surrender of your inner and outer being will bring this plasticity into all the parts of your nature;

consciousness will awaken everywhere in you by constant openness of wisdom and light and force, the harmony and beauty, the perfection that comes flowing down from above. Even the body will awake and unite at last its consciousness subliminal no longer to the supramental consciousness force, feel all Her powers permeating from above and below and around it and thrill to a supreme love and Ananda. But be on your guard and do not try to understand and judge the Divine Mother by your little earthly mind. The human mind shut in the prison of its half-lit obscurity cannot follow the many-sided freedom of the steps of the Divine Sakti. The rapidity and complexity of Her vision and action outrun its stumbling comprehension; the measures of Her movement are not its measurements.

Open rather your soul to Her and be content to feel Her with the psychic nature and see Her with the psychic vision that alone makes a straight response to the Truth. Avoid also the error of the ignorant mind's demand on the divine Powers to act always according to our crude surface notions of omniscience and omnipotence. For our mind clamours to be impressed at every hour by miraculous power and easy success and dazzling splendour; otherwise it cannot believe that here is the Divine. There are conditions that have been laid down by Supreme Will; there are many tangled knots that have to be loosened and cannot be cut abruptly asunder. The Divine Consciousness and Force are there to do at each moment the thing that is needed in the conditions of the labour, take always the step that is decreed and shape in the midst of imperfections the perfection that is to come. But only when the supermind has descended in you, She deals directly as the supramental Sakti with supramental natures. Follow your soul and not your mind; your soul that answers to the Truth, not the mind that leaps at appearances. Trust the Divine Power and She will free the godlike elements in you and shape all into an expression of Divine Nature; but that the change may arrive, take form and endure, there is needed the call from below with a will to recognise and not to deny the Light when it comes and there is needed the sanction of the Supreme from the above. The power that mediates between the sanction, and the call is the presence and power of the Divine Mother. The Mother's power and not any human endeavour and Tapasya can alone end the lid and tear the covering and shape the vessel and bring down Truth and Light and Life Divine and the Immortal Ananda into the world of obscurity, falsehood, death and suffering.

Om Santih Santih Santih!

6

ASSAMESE TANTRIKISM: ITS SIGNIFICANCE

(Sri Anwarul Hasan)

Like Malabar, Assam is the cradle of Hindu Tantrika philosophy and religion. In the Tantra Sastras, Kamarupa in Assam has been called the jewel of all sacred places. The famous temple of Goddess Kamakhya has attracted millions of devotees from all over India. In the texts of Tibetan Buddhism, translated by Dr. Evan-Wentz, there are evidences that many Lamas and Yogis from Tibet came to Kamarupa for initiation.

Assam was also reputed to be a land of occultism and psychical research. Among the common people of India 'the magic of Kamarupa' was famous. History tells us that one medieval Muslim divine and mystic, Hazrat Muhammad Gahuth, whose tomb is at Gwalior, went to Assam for the study of the Hindu Tantrika philosophy. The result of his researches he embodied in a Persian book, Abi-Hayat or the 'Water of Life.'

Tantrika philosophy, though often misunderstood, is a wonderful product of the spiritual genius of the Hindus. It is suited for subtle and philosophical minds. As it was not meant for the common masses, the initiates of Tantrikism expressed their doctrines in obscure and symbolic language. A knowledge of the following basic ideas will help to clear many misunderstandings. They are (a) Mother-worship, (b) Symbol of the subconscious mind, (c) Sex-symbols, (d) Idol-worship, (e) Kundalini Sakti.

We shall deal with these one by one:

MOTHER-WORSHIP

In the Tantrika philosophy God is worshipped in the form of the Divine Mother, or Devi. She is invoked by various names such as Lakshmi, Sarasvati, Maha Kali, Durga or Tripurasundari.

In the semitic religions, such as Islam, or Judaism, or Christianity, God is worshipped as Father. Mother-worship appears to the followers of these religions as something novel and strange.

In fact, the worship of the Divine Mother is older than the worship of God as Father. Essentially, God is neither male nor female. He is the absolute Reality. But human language is bound to express its ideas about Him in relative terms. Naturally, in a society where the father is the head of the family, and the child is accustomed to treat its father as the man in authority, it can easily imagine God in the form of a father.

But this kind of conception is of a later growth. Anthropological research shows that primitive man everywhere lived in a matriarchal society. In this kind of society, the wife or mother was the head of the family. The wife did not go to her husband's family after marriage, but the husband went and lived with the family of the wife. Such types of societies still exist in Malabar and are very common in Tibet. The renowned Sanskrit scholar and the erstwhile Sanskrit professor of the Leningrad University, Rahul Sankrityayan, has proved that among the ancient Aryans the matriarchal patterns of society did certainly exist.

It is in such societies that the worship of the Divine Mother was developed. This kind of worship became very popular and soothing to the mind, as none could exceed in the filial affection of the mother for her child. This conception was a great help to the devotee. Just as a child felt more at ease with its mother than its father, the devotee was also attracted to the Divine Mother than anything else. The absolute surrender of the soul became a main feature. Thus it is significant that in other forms of Hindu religion as well. Mother-worship is synthesised with the worship of God as Father. Sita and Rama, Radha and Krishna are worshipped together.

Devi-worship is a potent instrument for the removal of sex-cravings. The aspirant sees the Divine Mother in every female form and tries to maintain his attitude as such. Carnal emotions cannot thrive in this case, for anyone can imagine how sacred is the person of one's own mother.

The sacred word 'Om' is also a relic of the ancient Aryan Mother-worship. In every language of the world, the sound 'Ma' expresses the idea of mother, as for examples, in English, Mother; in Latin, mater; in Sanskrit, Matri; in French, mammon; in Persian, Madar; in Arabic, umm and so on. In fact, this sound comes to the child naturally while it is suckling at the breast of its mother. When it tries to make some sound, as the nose is obstructed by the bosom of its mother and the mouth engaged in suckling, the sound 'Ma' is produced.

The sacred Mantra 'Om' occurs in every religion of the world. In Christianity it occurs as Amen, in Islam as Amin. The Buddhists chant 'Om Mani Padme Hum.' Om is really a universal name for God.

SYMBOLS OF THE SUBCONSCIOUS MIND

The researches of modern psychoanalysis reveal and emphasise the great importance of symbols in the emotional life of man. Primitive man thought in symbols as he had no vocabulary to express abstract ideas and qualities. Before the alphabet was invented there was only picture-reading or writing. The ancient Egyptian 'Book of the Dead' is written in picture-symbols.

Modern psychology has shown that man has got two minds, the conscious mind and the subconscious mind. In the subconscious mind, all the memories of childhood and also all the experiences undergone by the human race since the dawn of history are treasured and stored up. It is the place of all our great feelings and emotions, as distinct from intellectual thoughts and reasonings. It is also the seat of telepathy, clairvoyance, hypnotism and other occult powers. In normal man the activity of the subconscious mind is shown in dreams.

The subconscious mind thinks entirely in symbols. While sleeping if some feeling of ambition is aroused, we dream that we are flying in the air; if there is some fear in our mind, we dream of demons and frightful animals, and so on. The subconscious mind is also influenced by the suggestion or repetition of the same idea again and again. It can also be influenced by loud sounds like ringing of bells or music.

The subsconscious mind can hardly be influenced by intellectual ideas.

Modern psychiatrists like Dr. Carl Gustav Jung have developed several systems of healing mental and nervous diseases by a careful study of the symbols of the subconscious mind as shown in dreams and hallucinations and attitudes created by past experiences of the patient. They have found that symbols are almost the only way to reach the subconscious mind of the patient, and to direct his emotions towards health and sanity.

The great symbols like the Cross, the Tau, the Svastika, the circle, etc., occur again and again in history.

SEX-SYMBOLS

The presence of sex-symbols in Hindu temples has drawn the criticism of various foreign writers who have not cared to delve deeper into the meaning of the objects. The phallus was the symbol for creative power in the primitive man. It is still so in the subconscious mind of the modern man. These symbols are found in all religions of the world, expressed differently. They represent God, the Creator. There is no vice in their symbology. It was a natural, straightforward and healthy imagination of the primitive man and his successors. There was nothing indecent, or immoral, or wicked bias in the minds of the simple, primitive people who created these symbols.

The normal sex-instinct can never be outright denounced or ignored. It can only be sublimated. By drawing our attention to the cosmic, creative aspect of the sex-instinct and by raising ourselves over the realms of physical desires, through discrimination, reflection and Yogic discipline the sex-instinct can be transmuted into spiritual energy. The Hindu Tantrik symbols are, therefore, intended for gradually converting the sex-desire into Ojas for spiritual attainments. They do not advocate suppression but sublimation.

IDOL-WORSHIP

Idols are of two kinds: (a) those representing the images of Jesus Christ, Buddha, Krishna, or Rama, whom the devotee believes to have been incarnations of God, and (b) those representing the symbolic image of some aspect of God, as for examples, Sarasvati (knowledge or learning), Lakshmi (wealth or beauty), and so on.

About the former class of idols there cannot be any philosophical difficulty. If the devotee believes them to have been Divine incarnations, he has a right to worship their images, exactly as he would have idolised them had they lived. Idolisation is not unknown among materialistic nations, as for examples, V.I. Lenin and J.V. Stalin. The utility of the latter class of symbols has already been explained. Indeed, symbols are much more powerful and effective in arousing the emotions of the subconscious mind than merely abstract, intellectual ideas: it is now a well-established truth of modern psychology.

Some semitic religions as Islam and Judaism forbid idol-worship because their prophets felt that the worship of the idea of God as an abstract entity was sufficient. But really the use of symbols is common to all religions. For example, in Islam and Judaism sacrifice of animals on certain occasions is permitted. The purpose, it is explained, is to bring to our mind the necessity of sacrificing ourselves our lower nature, to God. Even metaphysical ideas of God are in fact symbols, and without some kind of association or other, conception of God is not possible for the human mind.

There is another mystic reason for idol-worship. Thoughts are potential entities. They continue to remain in the subconscious mind and influence our conscious thoughts and attitudes. A devotee who worship Krishna or Rama is helped by the thought-forces of millions of devotees who have meditated upon and worshipped these divine symbols through centuries. Here the racial, traditional mind is touched.

The name of God is also a symbol. There must be some sort of association to capture our attention. If I invent a new name for God for myself, for example, AQB or P. 239, I shall not feel much religious emotion while uttering these names. If on the other hand I use a symbol which has been used by mankind for a long time as Allah or Krishna or some pleasant and sacred personality, I shall be easily inspired. The reason for this has already been explained.

Sankirtan, Namaz, Church choir, or simple repetition of the Lord's name also arouse the emotions of the subconscious mind. Religious music, the ringing of bells in temples, or the sonorous chants of Kalmas or psalms are definitely useful and almost universally necessary for the same purpose.

KUNDALINI SAKTI

Kundalini Yoga is the occult process for transmuting the physical energy into Ojas-Sakti. The human consciousness is taken through six different grades of perception until it merges in the Absolute. There is some direct evidence on this point coming from Tibetan systems of Yoga. Dr. Evans-Wentz has translated some Tibetan scriptures in his book Tibetan Yoga and Secret Doctrine, where the Hatha Yogic exercises, by which Lamas could endure the cold rigour of winters without any warm covering are described. The six Chakras or the plexi of the Kundalini Yoga and other Tantrik Yantras are ancient symbols of the subconscious mind. Some of these symbols have been deciphered independently by anthropologists and psychoanalysts like Dr. Jung (vide: The Integration of the Personality, C.G. Jung). The Yogic Kriyas and the processes of ascending the Kundalini Sakti have been described in detail by Swami Sivananda in his book, 'Kundalini Yoga.'

7

WORSHIP OF GÒD AS MOTHER

(Sri Anwarul Hasan)

The worship of God as the Divine Mother has been prevalent from times immemorial. Prof. Sigmond Freud says in his 'Totem and Taboo': "The great maternal deities have perhaps everywhere preceded the paternal deities." The ancient Egyptians worshipped Her under the name of Isis.

It would be a matter of great interest to the students of comparative religion to trace the parallel development of this idea in the Hindu and Christian Religions.

A brief outline of the Hindu ideas on this point may be given here in the inspiring words of Swami Sivananda Saraswati. "Mother-worship is the worship of God as the Divine Mother—Sri Mata. Her manifestations are countless. Durga, Kali, Bhagavati, Bhavani, Ambal, Ambika, Jagadamba, Kamesvari, Ganga, Uma, Chandi, Chamundi, Lalita, Gouri, Kundalini, Tara, Rajarajesvari, Tripurasundari etc. are all Her forms. Radha, Durga, Lakshmi, Sarasvati and Savitri are the five Prakritis. Though each name produces a specific result, yet it may also produce a general result. You may repeat any one of the names of the Devi. If you wish to obtain a particular fruit, you must invoke the Goddess by the corresponding name.

"The Upasana or worship of Devi, or Universal Mother leads to attainment of knowledge of the Self. It behoves, therefore, that the aspirant should approach the Mother first so that She may introduce Her spiritual child to the Father for its illumination or Self-realisation. That is why the devotees have placed Radha, Sita, Gouri first in the Yugala names viz., Radha Krishna, Sita Rama, Gouri Sankar, Uma Sankar, Bhavani Sankar, Lakshmi Narayana."

"Mother's grace is boundless. Her mercy is illimitable. Her knowledge is infinite. Her power is immeasurable. Her glory is ineffable. Her splendour is indescribable. She gives you Bhukti (material prosperity) and Mukti (liberation) also."

"The Kundalini Sakti is both cosmic and individual. The cosmic is called Maha Kundalini and the individual one the Kundalini. She lies dormant in the Muladhara Chakra in the form of a serpentine power or coiled up energy known as the Kundalini Sakti. She is at the centre of the life of the Universe. She is the primal force of life that underlies all existence. She vitalises the body through the Sushumna Nadi and nerves. She nourishes the body with chyle and blood. She vitalises the universe through Her energy."

"Worship of Devi in the form of Sri Vidya is of two kinds, viz., internal for advanced students and external for the less evolved students."

Practical instructions are given by Swami Sivananda for the external form of worship of Devi, in his book 'Ananda Lahari—Translation and Commentary':

"Get up in the morning at 4 a.m. Have your bath and other purificatory acts. Then perform your Nitya-karma in a separate Puja-room. Place therein the photos of your Ishta Devata, your Guru and that of Tripurasundari, the World-Mother and generatrix of this Universe in whose praise 'Ananda Lahari' is sung. After performing your Nitya-karma have a full reading of 'Ananda Lahari' with extreme faith and devotion. Keep a ghee-lamp burning throughout your Puja time. In the end, wave lights, burn incense and camphor before the Devi, your Ishta Devata and others. Place the offerings of coconut, honey, milk, fruits, etc., before the Deity and take the sacred Prasad. Do this regularly without fail.

"This will relieve you of all pains, miseries and tribulations. You will attain high position and success in life, and ultimately attain Sayujya Mukti also as stated in stanza 22. Pray to Mother Goddess with a melting heart with faith and devotion. I assure you, you will have rapid success in life and spiritual progress."

The internal form of worship of Devi is described by Swami Sivananda as follows: "In the internal form of worship there are neither rituals nor ceremonies. The Supreme Being in the form of Siva united with Sakti is worshipped at the various centres of energy of the human body or Chakras or lotuses. Those who perform the internal mode of worship believe in the identity of Siva and Sakti, in the awakening of Kundalini, and in taking it up through the various Chakras, to Sahasrara or the thousand-petalled lotus, through worship, Japa of Mantra, where the individual soul unites with the Supreme Soul.

"Saktism helps the aspirant to arouse the Kundalini and unite Her with Lord Siva and to enjoy the supreme bliss of Nirvikalpa Samadhi. When Kundalini sleeps man is awake to the world. He has objective consciousness. When She awakes, he sleeps. He loses all consciousness of the world and becomes one with the Lord. Mother Kundalini Sakti unites with Lord Siva in Sahasrara during Nirvikalpa Samadhi.

"The Yogi opens the mouth of Sushumna through Pranayama, Bandhas and Mudras and awakens the sleeping Kundalini or the primordial energy in Muladhara and takes it to Sahasrara at the crown of the head through the lower six Chakras. The lower six Chakras are the resting places or stages of Kundalini. He experiences different kinds of bliss and power at different centres. Ultimately Kundalini unites with Her Lord Parama Siva at Sahasrara. Now Nirvikalpa Samadhi takes place. The Yogi attains liberation and gets highest knowledge and bliss. The Yogi is tempted in the lower Chakras or resting places. He gets powers and various sorts of happiness.

He should try to reach his final or permanent abode, the Sahasrara. He should shun all Siddhis.

"Fearlessness, unruffled state of mind, dispassion, constant meditative mood, desirelessness, contentment, spiritual bliss, peace, inner spiritual strength, discrimination, self-restraint, one-pointedness of mind, strong faith in the existence of Isvara, and devotion are the signs that indicate that the Kundalini is awakened. Steadiness of mind, steadiness of Asana, purity, strong yearning for liberation, mercy, sweet voice, lustre in the eyes, peculiar glow in the face and charming personality are the marks of one whose Kundalini is awakened."

All the above quotations have been taken from Swami Sivananda's commentary on Ananda Lahari. In his 'Wisdom of Siva' he has thrown some further light on the subject of Kundalini Yoga.

"Sadhana, Dhriti, Sthirata, Dhairya, Laghava, Pratyaksha and Nirvikalpa Samadhi are the seven stages of Kundalini Yoga. When the Kundalini begins to rise upwards, the Yogic practitioner sees it as a beam of electric light."

Readers who are desirous of obtaining further information about the mysteries of Devi worship and the Sakta school of philosophy should read Swami Sivananda's English commentary on *Ananda Lahari*. *Ananda Lahari* is a devotional poem of forty-one stanzas by Sri Sankaracharya, containing beautiful hymns in praise of Devi or the Goddess Tripurasundari. In the words of Swami Sivananda, "Ananda Lahari is universally recognised as an ancient and authoritative Tantric work. There are thirty-five commentaries on this book. The stanzas contain various Mantras or mystic formulae, along with Yantras, or diagrams, for worship of Devi, and for the attainment of various Siddhis or powers. Worldly people generally use the verses of this hymn for invoking the Devi for the fulfilment of worldly desires."

The starting point of our research to trace the development of these ideas in the Christian religion is a paper by Dr. Ernest Jones, included in his "Essays in Applied Psycho-analysis," published in the International Psycho-analytical Library. In this paper, Dr. Ernest Jones draws our attention to the Christian Trinity, consisting of the Father, Son and Holy Ghost. He points out that it would be more reasonable to suppose that the third person in the Trinity the other two of which are the Father and Son should be the Mother and not the Holy Ghost. How then did the Holy Ghost come in?

Quoting various historical sources, Dr. Jones says that originally the Christian Trinity really consisted of the Father, Son and Mother (i.e., the Holy Virgin Mary, Mother of God). But later on, due to various historical reasons which need not be discussed here, the Semitic mind developed a repugnance to the idea of a female deity, and the Holy Ghost was substituted for the Divine Mother.

We shall not repeat the arguments of Dr. Jones, but shall try to find verification for his central thesis in other fields of human knowledge.

It is remarkable that, using another viewpoint of Depth-Psychology, Dr. Carl Gustav Jung arrives at the same conclusion. He says, in his Integration of Personality: "The femininity in the Godhead is kept secret and to say that the Holy Ghost is Sophia counts as a heresy. It was quite in line with this psychological fact when the Holy Ghost was taken as Sophia according to the heretical interpretation, for the Holy Ghost was mediator of the birth in the flesh, and thus made it possible for the luminous Godhead to become visible in the darkness of the world. It was this connection that aroused the suspicion that the Holy Ghost was feminine, for Mary was the dark earth of the field, *illa terra virgo nondum pluviis rigata* (that virgin soil not yet watered by the rains) as Augustine called her."

Dr. Jung says that he has found the feminine aspect of God recurring as a spiritual problem in the unconscious minds of his Christian patients. Let us summarise here some relevant characteristics of the Holy Ghost as it occurs in Christian literature.

(1) The feminine symbol of the dove is often used for the Holy Ghost in the Bible.

(2) The symbol of fire is also used for the Holy Ghost. The Holy Ghost is experienced as a Celestial Fire. On the day of Pentecost, the Holy Ghost came down on the Apostles in the form of 'tongue of fire.'

(3) The Holy Ghost confers seven spiritual gifts on the sincere believer. The Christian hymn says,

Come Holy Ghost our souls inspire
And lighten with Celestial Fire.
Thou the Holy Spirit Art—
Who dost thy sevenfold gifts impart.
Thy blessed unction from above,
Is comfort, peace and fire of love.

(4) The Holy Ghost, is experienced as a condition of great spiritual bliss and serenity. That is why it is called the Comforter in the Holy Bible. In the Christian hymns we find:

Come Holy Ghost, eternal God
Proceeding from above
Both from the Father and the Son,
The God of peace and love
Thou art the very Comforter
In grief and all distress
Thy heavenly comfort from on high
No tongue can it express.
The fountain and the living spring
Of joy celestial,
The fire so bright, the love so sweet
Thy unction spiritual.

But the four attributes of the Holy Ghost described above are the very same attributes we have found in our study of Kundalini Sakti. The Holy Ghost is a feminine symbol of God, and similarly the Kundalini Sakti is only an aspect of the Devi. She is the Cosmic Kundalini. Kundalini Yoga is simply the internal, philosophical mode of worshipping Devi.

Again, the Holy Ghost is represented by the symbol of fire, and as Swami Sivananda tells us, when the Kundalini begins to rise upward, the Yogic practitioner sees it as a beam of electric light. The Kundalini Sakti has also been called by some writers 'the Serpent Fire.'

The Kundalini Sakti passes through six lower Chakras and finally comes to the Seventh Centre, the Sahasrara. There are seven stages of Kundalini Yoga according to Swami Sivananda. Similarly the Holy Ghost confers seven spiritual gifts on mankind.

Both the Kundalini Sakti and the Holy Ghost, when experienced, lead to a feeling of spiritual joy, serenity of mind and divine ecstasy.

When the Kundalini rises, the Yogi gets various kinds of Siddhis or miraculous powers. Similarly Saint Paul tells us, in the Holy Bible that all kinds of gifts, like the gift of prophecy, the gift of healing etc., are conferred by the Holy Ghost.

Thus we find that the internal, philosophical mode of worshipping Devi as individual Kundalini Sakti indwelling within us, and the external ceremonial worship of Devi as Durga, Kali, Bhavani or Tripurasundari, which exist as one unified system of devotional thought in the Hindu religion, have become separated from each other in Christianity, the individual Kundalini being represented as the Holy Ghost, indwelling within us, and inspiring us to all good work, and the Cosmic Sakti or Devi being represented by the Holy Virgin Mary. These two parallel lines of thought which have become disconnected or torn out of their context in the Christian religion, are seen as two aspects of the same spiritual experience in the symmetrical and synthetic philosophy of the Tantras. Various puzzling problems of Christianity are solved in the light of Hindu mystical philosophy. The Holy Ghost is not only a substitute figure for the Virgin Mary, but is identical with Her.

Although the Holy Virgin, Mother of God, was left out from the Christian Trinity, the original tendency continued to assert itself in Christian thought. Let us make a brief historical survey of Mariolatry, or mystical devotion to Mary.

(1) Very early in the Christian Church, August 15th was fixed as the date of the Assumption of the Blessed Virgin, that is to say, of the miraculous passing of the Mother of the Lord. Juvenal, Bishop of Jerusalem, gives

the following account of the event (quoted in Smith's Dictionary of the Bible, article on Mary the Virgin, vol. II, page 269):

"From an ancient and most true tradition, we have received, that at the time of the glorious falling asleep of Holy Mary, Mother of God, all the holy apostles... borne aloft in a moment of time, came together to Jerusalem; and when they were near her they had a vision of angels... But after three days, on the angelic music ceasing, those of the apostles who were present opened the tomb, as one of them, Thomas, had been absent, and on his arrival wished to adore the body which has borne God. But her all glorious body they could not find... and they came to no other conclusion that He, who had chosen to take flesh of the Virgin Mary... was also pleased, after her departure, to honour her immaculate and unpolluted body with incorruption, and to translate her before the common resurrection of all men."

Some believed that she had never really died, but had been taken to God.

(2) Near about this time, the dogma of the Perpetual Virginity of the Holy Mary was also developed. This dogma means that not only there had been the Virgin Birth of Jesus Christ, the son of God, but also, that the so-called brothers of Jesus were not real brothers, but step-brothers.

(3) On December 8th, 1854, Pope Pius IX, by his Bull, 'Ineffable Deus' announced the Dogma of the Immaculate Conception of the Virgin Mary, to an Assembly of Bishops, at St. Peters, Rome. The Christian teaching asserts that all men, excepting Jesus Christ, are born with the taint of original sin. Jesus Christ is an

exception to this rule, as he was really an Incarnation of God. The dogma of the Immaculate Conception of Mary means that as the Son of God was born sinless, similarly His Holy Mother was free from original sin from her very birth, by a special decree of God.

These dogmas produced a state of mind in which the Virgin Mary came to be regarded as something akin to divine. It came to be believed that the son of God had made His Holy Mother Queen of Heaven, put all things under Her authority, and that She by Her powerful intercession with God, could bestow all kinds of benefits, both spiritual and material, on Her devotees. Or as Swami Sivananda says in his introduction to Ananda Lahari, "He has handed over the power of attorney to His consort Durga. It is Mother Durga only who looks after the affairs of the world."

Devotion to the Virgin Mary has produced some of the most beautiful kind of religious literature in the Christian Middle Ages. Let us study some of its aspects.

(1) The following Mantra is used by the Roman Catholic Christians when reciting the rosary, or the Christian Mala.

"Hail Mary, full of Grace, blessed art thou amongst women, and blessed is the fruit of thy womb, Jesus. Holy Mary, Mother of God, pray for us sinners now at the hour of Death, Amen."

The word 'rosary' refers to a legend. It is said that once a young monk was reciting the rosary. In a vision, the Virgin Mary was seen by his side, and as the words of the rosary came out of his mouth, they turned into roses, and the Blessed Virgin was seen weaving garlands out of them, and putting them on his head.

(2) It is the common practice with Roman Catholic Christians to begin a Novena to the Virgin Mary to get divine help when in distress. The Virgin Mary is invoked for nine days—hence it is called the Novena.

Says Swami Sivananda, "Do special Puja on Navarathri days. These nine days are very sacred to Devi. Plunge yourself in Her worship."

(3) Saint Therese of the Child Jesus was a great devotee of the Virgin Mary. In her Autobiography she writes how she once fell seriously ill in her girlhood, so that her life was despaired of, but she was miraculously cured by the Holy Virgin. We shall give the story in the words of the saint herself.

"Then looking towards the statue, she implored our Lady's assistance with all the fervour of a mother who begs the life of her child and will not be refused—and that cry of faith forced the gates of heaven

"Utterly exhausted, and finding no hope on earth, I too sought my Heavenly Mother's aid, and entreated her with all my heart to have pity on me.

"Suddenly the statue became animated and radiantly beautiful—with a divine beauty that no words of mine can ever convey. The look upon our Lady's face was unspeakably kind, sweet and compassionate, but what penetrated to the very depths of my soul was her gracious smile. Instantly all my pain vanished, my eyes filled, and big tears fell silently, tears of purest heavenly joy...

"When my sister saw me gaze fixedly on the statue, she said to herself: `Therese is cured.' It was true."

This story, which tells of the first ecstasy experienced by this great Christian Saint may well serve as an example, of the religious emotions felt by Christian devotees towards the Virgin Mary.

Various Christian mystics have expressed the feminine aspect of God. In 'Three Famous Occultists' W.P. Swainson gives a good summary.

"Our One-Twain Father-Mother God of which Harris speaks is essentially identical with the Will and Wisdom of Jacob Boehme, the Father and Mother of Anna Kingsford, Abha and Aima of the Kabalah, and Osiris and Isis of the old Egyptian Theosophy. In the most ancient times, the Supreme was symbolised by the letters I.O. signifying Father-Mother. All ancient religions taught the duality of the Divine nature, the feminine finding expression throughout the ages, under various names such as Isis, Sophia, Madonna, etc. Judaism has always esoterically taught the dual nature of the Supreme, while in the Roman Catholic Church we find this truth veiled under the worship of Virgin Mary." (pp. 183-184)

So let us offer our Prayer to the Divine Mother:

1. Hail Mary, Full of Grace, Blessed art Thou amongst women, and blessed is the fruit of Thy womb, Jesus. Holy Mary, Mother of God, pray for us sinners now and at the hour of death. Amen—*(The Christian Rosary)*

2. Our prostrations to Thee, O Devi, All Auspicious One, giver of success and prosperity, the abode of the helpless, the One with three eyes and of white colour, consort of Lord Narayana.

Adorations to the World-Mother who creates, preserves or sustains this universe through Her Sakti and bestows perennial joy and Supreme Peace to Her devotees. —*(Ancient Hindu Prayer)*

3. O Tripura Sundari! O Adorable Mother! I bow to Thee. Without Thy grace no one can get success in spiritual Sadhana and salvation in the end.

O Compassionate Mother! Thou art an ocean of mercy. Bless me. If I get a drop from that ocean, will it dry up?

O my sweet Mother! Guide me. Protect me. Save me. I am Thy child.

Jaya Tripura Sundari! Salutations.

—*(Swami Sivananda)*

4. Let all my idle talks be Japa sound divine
   All gesture be Mudra, all steps around Thy seat
   All lying down Pranam, all Homa what I eat
   All joy for the Supreme, for Thee all acts of mine.

—*(Ananda Lahari)*

5. Jaya Sri Durge, Jaya Sri Durge,

   Jaya Sri Durge Namah Om,

   Jaya Sri Durge, Jaya Sri Durge,

   Jaya Sri Durge Saranam Om,

   Jaya Sri Durge, Jaya Sri Durge,

   Jaya Sri Durge Pahimam,

   Jaya Sri Durge, Jaya Sri Durge,

   Jaya Sri Durge Rakshamam.

—*(Swami Sivananda)*

Book Two

NADA YOGA

INFLUENCE OF SOUND ON MIND

The deer is entrapped by sweet sound.

The cobra is enchanted by sweet music.

Raga Punnagavarali charms the cobra.

Nada entraps the mind.

The mind gets Laya in sweet Nada.

The mind is attracted by sweet Nada.

Therefore, you can easily control the mind

Through the practice of Nada Yoga.

GLORY OF NADANUSANDHAN

सदाशिवोक्तानि सपादलक्षलयावधानानि वसन्ति लोके ।
नादानुसन्धानसमाधिमेकं मन्यामहे मान्यतमं लयानाम् ॥

Sadasivoktani sapadalaksha-layavadhanani

vasanti loke,

Nadanusandhanasamadhimekam manyamahe

manyatamam layanam.

In this world there exist a lakh and a quarter types of Laya Sadhana, all told by Sadasiva. We consider the Nadanusandhana Samadhi as the best one among the various types of Layas.

नादानुसन्धान! नमोऽस्तु तुभ्यं त्वां मन्महे तत्त्वपदं लयानाम् ।
भवत्प्रसादात् पवनेन साकं विलीयते विष्णुपदे मनो मे ॥

Nadanusandhana namostu tubhyam

tvam manmahe tattvapadam layanam,

Bhavatprasadat pavanena sakam

vileeyate vishnupade mano me.

Nadanusandhana! May this salutation be unto thee. We hold you as the transcendent state in all Layas. We hold you as the transcandent state in all Layas. By your grace, my mind attains Laya in the abode of Vishnu, along with Prana.

सर्वचिन्तां परित्यज्य सावधानेन चेतसा ।
नाद एवानुसंधेयो योगसाम्राज्यमिच्छता ॥

Sarvachintam parityajya savadhanena chetasa,

Nada eva-anusandheyo yoga-samarajyam-icchata.

By one who is desirous of ataining perfection in Yoga, Nada alone has got to be closely heard (meditated upon), having abandoned all thoughts and with a calm mind.

—*Sankaracharya, 'Yoga-taravali.'*

नासनं सिद्धसदृशं न कुंभकसमं बलम् ।
न खेचरीसमा मुद्रा न नादसदृशो लयः ॥

Nasanam siddhasadrisam na kumbhakasamam

balam,

Na khechaareesama mudra na nada sadriso layah.

There is no Asana like Siddhasana, no strength like that of the Kumbhaka, no Mudra like the Khechari Mudra and no Laya like Nada. — *Sivasamhita*

NADA YOGA

Mokshapriya said:

O Swamiji! Please instruct me on Nada Yoga.

Swami Sivananda replied:

Nada is sound. Brahman willed. There was a Sat-Sankalpa. A vibration or Spandana arose. There was vibration of Om. This is Nada.

The mind is fixed on Nada or Anahata sounds are heard in the ear. It gets Laya or dissolution.The Yogi enters into Samadhi and atains Knowledge of the Self. This is Nada Yoga.

Nada Yoga is also called Laya Yoga.

Kundalini Yoga is also called Laya Yoga.

Mind is naturally attracted by sweet sounds. It is entrapped by the sweet sounds, just as a deer is entrapped by sweet music.

When the mind gets absorbed in the Anahata sounds, you will attain knowledge of hidden things. You will hear Para-Vak. You will develop the eye of intution. Eventually the mind is absorbed in Brahman or the Absolute.

Sit in Padmasana or Siddhasana or Sukhasana. Close the ears with the thumbs. This is Shanmukhi Mudra or Vaishnavi Mudra. Hear the Music of Anahata Sounds. Now you will have wonderful concentration.

Do Japa (Ajapa Japa) of Soham with breath or any Mantra. Practise Pranayama for one or two months. You will hear the ten sounds clearly and enjoy the music of the soul.

Abandon all worldly thoughts. Control your passion. Become indifferent to all objects. Practise Yama (self-restraint) or Sadachara (right conduct). Concentrate your attention on the Anahata sound which annihilates the mind.

GOAL OF LIFE

Life in the individual, in its ontological aspect is but a ceaseless striving after non-ending unalloyed bliss, eternal, immortal, perennial Bliss. Scriptures have proved it beyond doubt, Sages and Saints are voicing it forth ever since the dawn of creation that the Supreme Bliss can and should be had in one's own Self. Thus Self-realisation, Self-awareness or Self-Experience-Whole, Aparoksh-anubhuti is the *summum bonum* of human existence. That alone will bring to an end all our pains and miseries. But, how best are we to attain that?

Atmachaitanya Samadhi or Aparoksha Jnana is possible only when the mind becomes pure and Satvic. Purity of mind is had only when the little 'I', egoism or Ahamkara, is curbed, annihilated which means that I-ness and mine-ness have got to be abandoned. In turn, that involves purity and control of the Indriyas. Unless the mind is cultured and controlled, the Indriyas cannot be controlled. Thus, in a circular way, we come again to the mind. Rightly did the Sages exclaim: *Mana eva manushayanam karanam bandha-mokshayoh*—Mind alone is the cause for men's release and bondage.

Practical investigation in that direction has led the Sages to conclude that Prana and mind are inter-dependent in their functional abilities. As long as one remains uncontrolled, the other cannot be controlled. If one is under control, the other, too, comes under control of its own accord. It is not enough if they are simply controlled. As long as they are not annihilated, Vasanas will not leave us. Unless Vasanas are destroyed, Chitta cannot be destroyed. The destruction of Chitta alone can lead us to Jnana.

Thus we are left with two courses. Firstly to bring the Prana under control through various arduous Yogic processes, and then to control the mind and withdraw it from external objects and fix it on the Self. Secondly, we can try to annihilate the mind through effecting Mano-Laya by finding such a higher powerful principle towards which mind will naturally run and into which it will merge itself thus entering into a state of Laya. The Sages found that Mano-Laya followed by Mano-Nasa was a safer means to atain Self-realisation than the arduous process of controlling the mind and culturing it which is always attended by the danger of the mind jumping into the old grooves of Vasanas at any moment.

In the course of further practical investigations the Sages and Seers found that sound has the power to attract the mind and absorb it, so to say.

Thus Mano-Laya and Mano-Nasa through Nada Yoga (union or merger into Sound) was found to be an effective and safe means to Self-realisation.

POWER OF SOUND

Supercharged with transcendent soul-force, Sound is, in all creation, the one, powerful principle that widely influences and effectively brings under control all other manifestations. Many examples can be quoted to bear testimony to this claim of sound with reference to both the individual and the cosmos.

We have heard how Tansen was able to make it rain through the Megha Raga, how he lighted the lamp through singing in Deepaka Raga. There are, again certain accounts relating to the Tibetan Lamas, which tell us how the Lamas drove away and dispersed rain-bearing clouds, or gathered the clouds and made them to rain by blowing the horns and the trumpets and beating the drums.

We have also seen how the deer or the cobra gets lured through sweet music. That act of theirs at the pre-rational level clearly shows that there exists a certain relationship between sound and mind and that the mind naturally runs towards sound and in doing so, forgets the external world altogether. There thus being a natural tendency in all creation to find solace and peace in sound, at the rational level we can only do the same with better effieciency and result, and we do.

How many persons in the work-a-day world drown their worldly miseries and pain sweet rhythmic music? Even an ignorant man who knows not the A,B,C of music stands spell-bound, as though, through some magic, when he hears some sweet melodious music. That goes only to prove that in the presence of rhythmic sound, mind refuses to think about anything other than the sound.

The ignorant man exclaims after hearing some nice music 'I enjoyed it well. I know nothing' and that exclamation is almost identical with that of the man who exclaims, 'I slept well, I knew nothing'. That clearly proves that mind was enjoying a state of oneness with sound, just like its attaining Laya in causal ignorance during deep sleep.

All these things only show us the superiority of Sound over our minds, and the unshakable basis of Nada Yoga and the usefulness of Sound in effecting Mano-Laya.

SOUND AND BRAHMAN

Sound is the first manifestation of the Absolute.

We know not anything about the nature of the Absolute as it exists except that It *is*. With all their kindness, the Scriptures have tried to tell us all about the creation, how it proceeded from the Absolute. They say: Brahman was one and non-dual. It thought, *'Ekoham, Bahu syam'.* That caused a vibration eventually bringing in Sound and that Sound was Om, whence are all other manifestations.

From that we can say, as an inference: As long as the force of the Brahma-Sankalpa lasts, there exists the cosmic vibration and the Sound. When the vibration ceases the Sound also disappears into the transcendental Being. During the vibrant stage creation proceeds, the elements and the Tanmatras are successively born from the previous ones, and finally quintuplication takes place and we have the world as we see it. During the cessation of the vibration, the reverse takes place and there is involution, all this world disappearing into sound and sound disappearing into Brahman.

Thus, Sound is virtually the comprehensible basis for all creation. Naturally, therefore, it has the power to absorb the other manifestations.

Brahman is incomprehensible in Its transcendent aspect. The nearest approach to It is only Sound, or we can call Sound as Aparam Brahma.

ANAHATA SOUND

As in the macrocosm, so too, in the microcosm.

All that is told of the Universe and cosmic creation, can be applied in toto to the individual.

Our physical and astral bodies, our Indriyas and the mind, all should have Sound as their basis. As we penetrate deep into them they should only lead us to Sound. As we analyse our individual existence, it should take us to Sound before we reach the transcendent Self.

Idaikkattu Chittar, a South Indian Mystic, says in effect: "Before the sound in you gets involved, know the substratum of Omkar."

It clearly indicates that there exists a certain sound within us supporting all our activities and that when once that sound gets involved into its cause, our present earthly life comes to an end.

What can it be other than the Sound that is the first manifestation of our Self before it appears as the mind and the Indriyas?

Normally, when we plug our both ears and try to listen within us, we shall hear this wonderful Sound which goes by the name Anahata Sound.

Anahata literally means unbeaten, unstruck. Anahata Sound is so called because it is not the result of striking or beating certain things like the raising of a note on the violin or the Vina. It comes from the Anahata Chakra. Because the Anahata Sound comes from that Chakra, the Chakra is so named.

Sound, as it ought to, forms the basis in all the six chakras inside our body. In the lower three Chakras, it is not heard clearly since they are controlled by the Tattvas—earth, fire and water respectively from Muladhara.

Vayu Tattva predominates the Anahata Chakra. So we are able to hear clearly and distinctly various sounds at the Anahata Chakra, the nature of the sound differeing according to the disturbance caused by the motion of Vayu Tattva. At this Chakra, we can hear both the Sthula and Sukshma sounds, and it depends upon the intensity of our concentration and the quietude in the Tattva.

MANO-LAYA TO BE SOUGHT ONLY IN THE ANAHATA SOUND

It is not impossible for us to effect Mano-Laya in external music. But it will not lead us to our goal. Mano-Laya is only a means, whereas our goal is our own self. Merging the mind in external sounds can only be *compared* to deep sleep. It cannot help us with Mano-Nasa.

Seeking Mano-Laya in the Anahata Sound is doubly effective. Just like the child running automatically towards its mother, the mind will quickly run towards the Anahata Sound since the latter is the basis for the mind. Like the child getting into a state of oneness with the mother very quickly, the mind too will enter into state of Laya in the Anahata Sound. Secondly, by doing so, by effecting the union of mind with the Anahata Sound, we will be actually causing the effect to disappear into the cause or, in other words, there will be Mano-Nasa.

Getting ourselves established first in the Anahata Sound and then going to our own Self is but a form of Krama Mukti.

Anahata sounds or the melody, are the mystic sounds heard by the Yogi at the beginning of his cycle of meditation. This subject is termed Nada Anusandhana or an enquiry into the mystic sounds. This is a sign of purification of the Nadis or astral currents, due to Pranayama. The sounds can also be heard after the uttering of the Ajapa Gayatri Mantra, 'Hamsa Soham', a lakh of times. The sounds are heard through the right ear with or without closing the ears. The sounds are distinct when heard through closed ears. The ears can be closed by introducing the two thumbs into the ears through the process of Yoni Mudra. Sit on Padma or Siddha Asana, close the ears with right and left thumbs, and hear the sounds very attentively. Occasionally, you can hear the sounds through the left ear also. Practise to hear from the right ear only. Why do you hear through the right ear only or hear distinctly through the right ear? Because of the influence of the Solar Nadi, Pingala, on the right side of the nose. The Anahata sound is also called Omkara Dhvani. It is due to the vibration of Prana in the heart.

TEN KINDS OF SOUNDS

Nada that is heard is of 10 kinds. The first is Chini (like the sound of that word Chini); the second is Chini-Chini; the third is the sound of bell; the fourth is that of conch; the fifth is that of Tantri (lute); the sixth is the sound of Tala (cymbals); the seventh is that of flute; the eighth is that of Bheri (drum); the ninth is that of Mridanga (double drum) and the tenth is that of clouds, viz., thunder.

VOICE OF THE SILENCE

"Before thou settest thy foot upon the ladder's upper rung, the ladder of the mystic sounds, thou hast to hear the voice of thy inner God (Higher Self) in seven manners. The first is like the nightingale's sweet voice chanting a song of parting to its mate. The second comes as the sound of a silver cymbal of the Dhyanis, awakening the twinkling stars. The next is as the plaint melodious of the ocean spirit imprisoned in its shell. And this is followed by the chant of Vina. The fifth is like sound of a bamboo-flute shrills in thine ear. It changes next into a trumpet-blast. The last vibrates like the dull rumbling of a thunder-cloud. The seventh swallows all the other sounds. They die, and then are heard no more."

LAYA YOGA
(Concentration on Anahata Sounds)

Dharana is the intense and perfect concentration of the mind upon some one interior or exterior object or sounds like Anahata sounds or any abstract idea, accompanied by complete abstraction (Pratyahara) from everything pertaining to the external universe, or the world of senses.

Sit on Padma or Siddha Asana. Practrise Yoni Mudra by closing the ears with the thumbs. Hear the internal sound through the right ear. The sound which you hear will make you deaf to all external sounds. Having overcome all obstacles, you will enter the Turiya state within 15 days. In the beginning of your priactice, you will hear many loud sounds. They gradually increase in pitch and are heard more and more subtly. You should try to distinguish sounds more and more subtle. You may change your concentration from the gross sound to the subtle, or from the subtle to the gross, but you should not allow your mind to be diverted from them towards other objects.

The mind having at first concentrated itself on any one sound, fixes itself firmly to that and is absorbed in it. The mind becoming insensible to the external impressions becomes one with the sound as milk with water and then becomes rapidly absorbed in Chidakasa (the Akasa where Chit prevails). Being indifferent towards all objects, you, having controlled the passions, should by continual practice concentrate your attention upon the sound which destroys the mind. Having abandoned all thoughts and being freed from all actions, you should always concentrate your attention on the sound, and then your Chitta becomes absorbed in it. Just as the bee drinking the honey alone does not care for the odour, so, the Chitta, which is always absorbed in sound does not long for sensual objects, as it is bound by the sweet smell of the Nada and has abandoned its flitting nature. The serpent Chitta through listening to the Nada, is entirely absorbed in it, and becoming unconscious of everything, concentrates itself on the sound. The sound serves the purpose of a sharp goad to control the maddened elephant—Chitta which roves in the pleasure-garden of the sensual objects. It serves the purpose of a snare for binding the deer—Chitta. It also serves the purpose of a shore to the ocean-waves of Chitta. The sound proceeding from Pranava, which is Brahman, is of the nature of effulgence; the mind becomes absorbed in it; that is the supreme seat of Vishnu. The mind exists so long as there is sound, but with its cessation, there is that state termed Turiya. This sound is absorbed in Brahman and the soundless state is the supreme seat. The mind which along with Pranava has its Karmic affinities destroyed by the constant concentration upon Nada is absorbed in the unstained One. There is no doubt of it. Being freed from all states and all thoughts whatever, you will remain like one dead. You will become a Mukta. There is no doubt about this. The body is certainly like a log and does not feel heat or cold, joy or sorrow. When the spiritual sight becomes fixed without any object to be seen, when the Prana becomes still without any effort, and when the Chitta becomes firm without any support, you become Brahman, (Brahmavid Brahman).

You may experience the tenth sound without the first nine sounds through the initiation of a Guru. In the first stage, the body become Chin-chini; in the second, there is the (Bhanjana) breaking or affecting in the body; in the third, there is the (Bhedana) piercing; in fourth, the head shakes; in the fifth, the palate produces saliva; in the sixth, nectar is attained; in the seventh, the knowledge of the hidden things in the world arises; in the eighth, Paravak is heard; in the ninth, the body becomes invisible and the pure divine eye is developed; in the tenth, you attain the state of Para Brahman. When Manas is destroyed when virtues and sins are burnt away, you shine as the effulgent, immaculate, eternal, stainless, Suddha Brahman. Om.

SOUND AND IMAGE

Sounds are vibrations. They give rise to definite forms. Each sound produces a form in the invisible world and combinations of sound create complicated shapes.

The text-books of science describe certain experiments which show that notes produced by certain instruments trace out on a bed of sand definite geometrical figures. It is thus demonstrated that rhythmical vibrations give rise to regular geometrical figures. The Hindu books on music tell us that the various musical tunes, 'Ragas' and 'Raginis', have each a particular shape, which these books graphically describe. For instance, the Megha-Raga is said to be a majestic figure seated on an elephant. The Vasanta-Raga is described as a beautiful youth decked with flowers. All this means that a particular Raga or Ragini, when accurately sung, produces etheric vibrations which create the particular shape, said to be the characteristic of it. This view has recently received corroborations from the experiments carried on by Mrs.Watts Hughes, the gifted author of 'Voice Figures'. She delivered an illustrated lecture before a select audience in Lord Leighton'a studio to demonstrate the beautiful scientific discoveries on which she had alighted, as the result of many years' patient labour. Mrs.Hughes sings into a simple instrument called an 'Eidophone' which consists of a tube, a receiver and a flexible membrane, and she finds that each note assumes a definite and constant shape, as revealed through a sensitive and mobile medium. At the outset of her lecture, she placed tiny seeds upon the flexible membrane and the air vibrations set up by the notes she sounded danced them into definite geometric patterns. Afterwards she used dusts of various kinds, copodium dust being found particularly suitable. A reporter, describing the shape of the notes, speaks of them as remarkable revelations of geometry, perspective and shading; "Stars, spirals, snakes and imaginations rioting in a wealth of captivating methodical design." Such were what were first shown. Once when Mrs. Hughes was singing a note, a daisy appeared and disappeared and "I tried", she said, "to sing it back for weeks before; at last I succeeded." Now she knows the precise inflections of the particular note that is a daisy, and it is made constant and definite by a strange method of coaxing an alteration of crescendo and diminendo. After the audience had gazed enraptured, a series of daisies, some with succeeding rows of petals, delicately viewed, they were shown other notes and these were daisies of great beauty. "How wonderful! How lovely!" were the audible exclamations that arose from the late Lord Leighton's studio, an exquisite form succeeded exquisite form on the screen! The flowers were followed by sea-monsters, serpentine forms of swelling rotundity, full of light and shade and details, feeding in miles of perspective. After these notes came there from other trees, trees with fruits falling, trees with a fore-ground of rocks, trees with sea behind. "Why", exclaimed the people in the audience, "they are just like Japanese landscapes."

While in France, Madam Finlang's singing of a hymn to Virgin Mary 'O Ave Marium' brought out the form of Mary with child Jesus on her lap and again the singing of a hymn to 'Bhairava' by a Bengali student of Benares studying in France, gave rise to the formation of the figure of Bhairava with his vehicle, the dog.

Thus repeated singing of the Name of the Lord builds up gradually the form of the Devata or the special manifestation of the Deity whom you seek to worship, and this acts as a focus to concentrate the benign influence of the Divine Being, which, radiating from the centre, penetrates the worshipper.

When one enters the state of meditation, the flow of the inner Vritti is greatly intensified. The deeper one goes into meditation the more marked is the effect. The concentration of the mind upwards sends a rush of this force through the top of the head and the response comes in a fine rain of soft magnetism. The feeling arising from the downward power sends a wonderful glow through the body, and one feels as if he is bathed in a soft kind of electricity.

The above experiments demonstrate the following facts: 1. Sounds produce shapes. 2. Particular notes give rise to particular forms. 3. If you want to generate a particular form, you must produce a definite note in a particular pitch.

The repetition of the Panchakshara Mantra, 'Om Namah Sivaya,' produces the form of Lord Siva. The repetition of 'Om Namo Narayanaya,' the Ashtakshara Mantra of Vishnu, produces the form of Vishnu. In a Mantra, the vibrations to be produced by the notes are all important. Much emphasis is laid on the pitch (Svara) as well as form (Varna) of a Mantra. Varna literally means colour. In the invisible world all sounds are accompanied by colours, so that they give rise to many-hued shapes. In the same way colours are accompanied by sounds. A particular note has to be used to produce a particular form. Different notes in different pitches give rise to different shapes. In the science of Mantras, we use different Mantras for the purpose of invoking different gods. If you worship Lord Siva you use 'Om Namah Sivaya', but in worshipping Vishnu or Sakti you will have to change the Mantra. What hapapens when a Mantra is recited? The repated recitation of the Mantra produces in the mind the form of the Devata or the Deity connected with the Mantra which is your Ishta, and this form becomes the centre of your consciousness when you directly realise it. It is, therefore, said that the Mantra of the Deva is the Deva Himself. This may explain the much misunderstood dictum of the Mimamsa philosophers that the gods do not exist apart from the Mantras (*Mantratmako Devah*). This really means that when a paritcular Mantra appropriate to a particular god is properly recited, the vibrations so set up create in the higher planes a special form which that god ensouls for the time being.

THE FOUR STAGES OF SOUND

The Vedas form the sound-manifestation of Isvara. That sound has four divisions, Para which finds manifestation only in Prana, Pasyanti which finds manifestation in the mind, Madhyama which finds manifestation in the Indriyas and Vaikari which finds manifestation in articulate expression.

Articulation is the last and grossest expression of divine sound energy. The highest manifestation of sound energy, the primal voice, the divine voice, is Para. The Para voice becomes the root-ideas or germ-thoughts. It is the first manifestation of voice. In Para the sound remains in an undifferentiated form. Para, Pasyanti, Madhyama and Vaikhari are the various gradations of sound. Madhyama is the intermediate unexpressed state of sound. Its seat is the heart.

The seat of Pasyanti is the navel or the Manipura Chakra. Yogins who have subtle inner vision can experience the Pasyanti state of a word which has colour and form, which is common for all languages and which has the vibrating homogeneity of sound. Indians, Europeans, Americans, Africans, Japanese, birds, beasts—all experience the same Bhavana of a thing in the Pasyanti state of voice or sound. Gesture is a sort of mute subtle language. It is one and the same for all persons. Any individual of any country will make the same gesture by holding his hand to his mouth in a particular manner when he is thirsty. As one and the same power of Sakti working through the ears become hearing, through the eyes become seeing and so forth, the same Pasyanti assumes different forms of sound when materialised. The Lord manifests Himself through His Mayaic power first as Para Vani at the navel, then as Madhyama in the heart and then eventually as Vaikari in the throat and mouth. This is the divine descent of His voice. All the Vaikari is His voice only. It is the voice of the Virat Purusha.

WHAT IS NADA?

Nada is Siva-Sakti. The union and mutual relation of Siva and Sakti is Nada. From Nada came Mahabindu. Nada is action. Sakti-tattva becomes for the first time active as Nada.

Nada etymologically means sound. Sound is not the gross sound which is heard by the ear. Nada is the most subtle aspect of Sabda. Nada develops into Bindu.

NADA, BINDU AND KALA

An aspirant enquires: "I would like to ask you to enlighten me on the maning of the words, Nada, Bindu and Kala, as they are used in Hatha Yoga Pradipika, where it is said that Siva appears as Nada, Bindu and

Kala. How can Siva, who is the Supreme Reality, devoid of any quality, possess Kala which represents a particular Guna or quality?

The primal sound or first vibration from which all creation has emanated is Nada. It is the first emanative stage in the projection of the universe (creation). Nada is the first manifestation of the unmanifested Absolute. It is Omkara or Sabda-Brahman. It is also mystic inner sound on which the Yogi concentrates.

Bindu is not to be taken in the sense of drop or vital force. It is the inconceivable, subtle point, the very root of all manifestation. It is the point from which is projected the phenomenal universe of names and forms. From this point or Bindu emanates all creation. Therefore, in its aspect as the vital source of manifestation, it is sometimes used in a sense akin to vital force.

Briefly put in its primary sense, Kala means a particular kind of divine power of quality (Guna). There is no question of Kala, in the case of Parama-Siva, who is Nirguna, without quality, and therefore Kalateeta. The moment Sakti manifests, the Absolute Siva Tattva becomes present in His Saguna aspect which is also Sa-kala. When thus manifest, He is Purnakalamurti, endowed with sixteen Kalas. He who possesses one of these sixteen Kalas is called a Kalamurti; further fraction of this becomes Amshamurti, and still further fraction is sometimes called Amshamshamurti.

DHVANI

In certain sounds such as the beating of a drum, the roar of thunder, the sounds of laughing, crying, etc., no letters are manifested. This is Dhvani. In certain others, letters or Varnas are manifested as in the case of sounds of articulate speech. This is Varnatmaka Sabda.

Sound is produced by the contact of one thing with another, of the hand and the drum in the case of unlettered sound and the vocal organs and ear in the case of uttered speech.

But the Anahata sound is uncreated and self-produced. It is not caused by the striking of one thing against another.

Varnatmaka Sabda has a meaning. Every Dhvani also has a meaning. The sound of laughing indicates that a particular person is happy. The sound of crying indicates that a particular person is in trouble. The sound of a bell indicates that tea or food is ready. The sound of a bugle indicates that there is a parade.

NADANUSANDHAN

(Practical Sadhana)

Nadanusadhanam means meditation on Nada or Sound that is heard at the Anahata Chakra.

The essential prereqisites for this type of Sadhana are the same as those for any other Yoga Sadhana. Ethical and moral preparations are the first important prerequisites. Similarly, proficiency in Hatha Yoga and Pranayama is essential. It is better to have sufficient practice in concentration and meditation. That will make it easy for us to concentrate inwardly and meditate on the Anahata sounds. Ajapa Japa or Japa of 'Soham' with breath will help you in your concentration on the subtle sounds. That by itself will take you to the Anahata sound.

Sit in Padmasana or Siddhasana. Have the Shanmukhi or the Vaishnavi Mudra. (Details about this can be had from my book 'Hatha Yoga'.) Do Ajapa Japa. Let your gaze be inwards. That will lead you to the Anahata sound.

With Shanmukhi Mudra in Padmasana or Siddhasana, you can also lead the Prana and Apana into the Sushumna and then meditate on the Anahata Chakra. Then also, you will hear the Anahata sounds. The sweet melody of the sounds will bestow on you greater power of concentration.

At first you will hear ten different sounds that will make you deaf to all external sounds. The sounds are: Chini, Chin-chini, ringing of the bell, blowing the conch, sound of the lute, sound of the cymbal, that of the flute, like that of a drum, of a Mridanga and that of the thunder. These sounds should be heard through the right ear.

There are two aspects of these sounds, gross and subtle. You should proceed from the gross ones to the subtle ones. If the mind runs only towards the gross sounds, do not get perturbed. Let it get first accustomed to and established in the gross sound. Then it can be led to the subtle sound.

Bear in mind that Mano-Laya is not the goal but that Mano-Nasa and Self-realisation is the goal.

Remember not to take any special fancy or liking for any particular sound but try to lead the mind from the first to the second, from the second to the third, and so on to **the tenth.**

There is another school of Nada Yoga that distinguishes three different stages in the hearing of the sounds.

The first stage is when the Prana and Apana are led near the Brahmarandhra. The second stage comes when they enter the Brahmarandhra and the third when they are well-established in it. During the first stage, sounds like that of the roaring sea, the beating of drums, etc., are heard. During the second, sounds like those of Mridanga, conch, etc., are heard. In the third stage, sounds like Kinkini, humming of the bee, sound of the flute or the lute etc., are heard.

Knowledge pertaining to hidden things arise in a person who can hear well the seventh sound (like that of the flute). If he can hear clearly the eighth sound, then he will hear Para Vak. With the ninth, he develops the Divine Eye. When he hears th tenth, he verily attains Para-Brahman.

RELEASE OR MOKSHA

The mind that is attracted by the Anahata sound shall surely atain the state of Samadhi. Just like a bee that tastes the sweet honey is not attracted by the smell of the flower, the mind too shall no more run after the old Vasanas if once it hears the subtle Anahata sound. The mind-cobra hearing the Anahata sound stands spell-bound shaking all Vasanas and wavering nature. Forgetting the external sense-world, it gets one-pointed, and never wanders about thereafter.

The sound that is the nature of Om or Pranava which is Brahman itself, is of the form of Effulgence. That is the

Supreme Abode of Lord Vishnu. In that mind atains Laya. That means Moksha.

As long as the sounds (Anahata) are heard, so long there exists the Akasa Tattva in the mind. As long as the Anahata sound is heard, the mind exists. When once the Anahata sound becomes Soundless Sound, Brahmanubhuti or Atmanubhuti prevails.

The Nada with sound dissolves into the Akshara Brahman. That Soundless Sound alone is called the Supreme Abode. When the mind leaving the subtle sound goes to the Soundless Sound, the mind and Prana enter into a state of Laya in the Nirakara Brahman.

The mind that has become one with Nada like milk in water enters the Chidakasa alongwith the Nada. There, at that moment, the tenth sound, Thunder, prevails for a while; then like lightning the Supreme Effulgence reveals its nature at which moment the thunder-like sound becomes Soundless Sound, Brahma-Jnana or Atma-Jnana dawns.

THE SACRED PRANAVA

SACRED OM

Om is the word of power,
Om is the sacred monosyllable,
Om is the mystic letter,
Om is the Immortal Akshara.

In Om the world rests,
In Om we live and move,
In Om we go to rest,
In Om we find our quest.

Sing Om rhythmically,
Chant Om loudly,
Roar Om forcibly,
Repeat Om mentally.

Draw strength from Om,
Get inspiration from Om,
Derive energy from Om,
Imbibe bliss from Om.

Glory to Om,
Victory to Om,
Hosanna to Om,
Hail to Om.

Adorations to Om,
Salutations to Om,
Prostrations to Om
Devotion to Om.

Rely on Om,
Reflect on Om,
Concentrate on Om,
Meditate on Om.

Om!   Om!   Om!

SWEET OM

Om is the word of power,
Om is the sacred monosyllable,
Om is the highest Mantra,
Om is the symbol of Brahman,
Om is Soham,
Om is Om Tat Sat.
Om is the source of everything,
Om is the womb of Vedas,
Om is the basis for languages,

In Om merge all Trinities,
From Om proceed all sounds,
In Om exist all objects.
O Sweet Om! Potent Pranava!
The Life of my life,
The boat to cross this Samsara,
Harbinger of Eternal Bliss,
My Redeemer and Saviour!
Guide me and take me
To Brahman, the hidden sage!

NADA IS SOUND

Nada is sound.
Om is Nada Brahman.
Veda is Nada Brahman.
Sound is vibration.
Name is inseparable from form.
The form may vanish,
But the name or sound remains.
Om is the first vibration of sound.
The world has come out of Nada or Om.
In Pralaya all sounds merge in Om.
Sound vibration is gross and subtle.
The quality of Akasa is sound.
Akasa is infinite.
So you can fill the ear with the infinite sound.

नादबिन्दूपनिषत्

वैराजात्मोपासनया संजातज्ञानवह्निना ।
दग्ध्वा कर्मत्रयं योगी यत्पदं याति तद्भजे ॥

ॐ वाङ्मे मनसीति शान्तिः ।

ओम् अकारो दक्षिणः पक्ष उकारस्तूत्तरः स्मृतः ।
मकारं पुच्छमित्याहुरर्धमात्रा तु मस्तकम् ॥१॥

पादादिकं गुणास्तस्य शरीरं तत्त्वमुच्यते ।
धर्मोऽस्य दक्षिणं चक्षुरधर्मोऽथो परः स्मृतः ॥२॥

भूर्लोकः पादयोस्तस्य भुवर्लोकस्तु जानुनि ।
सुवर्लोकः कटीदेशे नाभिदेशे महर्जगत् ॥३॥

जनो लोकस्तु हृद्देशे कण्ठे लोकस्तपस्ततः ।
भ्रुवोर्ललाटमध्ये तु सत्यलोको व्यवस्थितः ॥४॥

सहस्रार्णमतीवात्र मन्त्र एष प्रदर्शितः ।
एवमेतां समारूढो हंसयोगविचक्षणः ॥५॥

न भिद्यते कर्मचारैः पापकोटिशतैरपि ।
आग्नेयी प्रथमा मात्रा वायव्येषा तथापरा ॥६॥

भानुमण्डलसंकाशा भवेन्मात्रा तथोत्तरा ।
परमा चार्धमात्रा या वारुणी तां विदुर्बुधाः ॥७॥

कालत्रयेऽपि यस्येमा मात्रा नूनं प्रतिष्ठिताः ।
एष ओंकार आख्यातो धारणाभिर्निबोधत ॥८॥

धोषिणी प्रथमा मात्रा विद्या मात्रा तथापरा ।
पतङ्गिनी तृतीया स्याच्चतुर्थी वायुवेगिनी ॥९॥

पञ्चमी नामधेया तु षष्ठी चैन्द्र्यभिधीयते ।
सप्तमी वैष्णवी नाम अष्टमी शांकरीति च ॥१०॥

नवमी महती नाम धृतिस्तु दशमी मता ।
एकादशी भवेन्नारी ब्राह्मी तु द्वादशी परा ॥११॥

प्रथमायां तु मात्रायां यदि प्राणैर्वियुध्यते ।
भारते वर्षराजासौ सार्वभौमः प्रजायते ॥१२॥

द्वितीयायां समुत्क्रान्तो भवेद्यक्षो महात्मवान्।
विद्याधरस्तृतीयायां गान्धर्वस्तु चतुर्थिका॥१३॥

पञ्चम्यामथ मात्रायां यदि प्राणैर्वियुज्यते।
उषितः सह देवत्वं सोमलोके महीयते॥१४॥

षष्ठ्यामिन्द्रस्य सायुज्यं सप्तम्यां वैष्णवं पदम्।
अष्टम्यां व्रजते रूद्रं पशूनां च पतिं तथा॥१५॥

नवम्यां तु महर्लोकं दशम्यां तु जनं व्रजेत्।
एकादश्यां तपोलोकं द्वादश्यां ब्रह्म शाश्वतम्॥१६॥

ततः परतरं शुद्धं व्यापकं निर्मलं शिवम्।
सदोदितं परं ब्रह्म ज्योतिषामुदयो यतः॥१७॥

अतीन्द्रियं गुणातीतं मनो लीनं यदा भवेत्।
अनूपमं शिवं शान्तं योगयुक्तं सदाविशेत्॥१८॥

तद्युक्तस्तन्मयो जन्तुः शनैर्मुञ्चेत्कलेवरम्।
संस्थितो योगचारेण सर्वसङ्गविवर्जितः॥१९॥

ततो विलीनपाशोऽसौ विमलः कमलाप्रभुः।
तेनैव ब्रह्मभावेन परमानन्दमश्नुते॥२०॥

आत्मानं सततं ज्ञात्वा कालं नय महामते।
प्रारब्धमखिलं भुञ्जन्नोद्वेगं कर्तुमर्हसि॥२१॥

उत्पन्ने तत्त्वविज्ञाने प्रारब्धं नैव मुञ्चति।
तत्त्वज्ञानोदयादूर्ध्वं प्रारब्धं नैव विद्यते॥२२॥

देहादीनामसत्त्वातु यथा स्वप्ने विबोधतः।
कर्म जन्मान्तरीयं यत्प्रारब्धमिति कीर्तितम्॥२३॥

तत्तु जन्मान्तराभावात्पुंसो नैवास्ति कर्हिचित्।
स्वप्नदेहो यथाध्यास्तस्थैवायं हि देहकः॥२४॥

अध्यास्तस्य कुतो जन्म जन्माभावे कुतः स्थितिः ।
उपादानं प्रपञ्चस्य मृद्भाण्डस्येव पश्यति ॥२५॥

अज्ञानं चेति वेदान्तैस्तस्मिन्नष्टे क्व विश्वता ।
यथा रज्जुं परित्यज्य सर्पं गृह्णाति वै भ्रमात् ॥२६॥

तद्वत्सत्यमविज्ञाय जगत्पश्यति मूढधीः ।
रज्जुखण्डे परिज्ञाते सर्परूपं न तिष्ठति ॥२७॥

अधिष्ठाने तथा ज्ञाते प्रपञ्चे शून्यतां गते ।
देहस्यापि प्रपञ्चत्वात्प्रारब्धावस्थितिः कुतः ॥२८॥

अज्ञानजनबोधार्थं प्रारब्धमिति चोच्यते ।
ततः कालवशादेव प्रारब्धे तु क्षयं गते ॥२९॥

ब्रह्मप्रणवसन्धानं नादो ज्योतिर्मयः शिवः ।
स्वयमाविर्भवेदात्मा मेघापायेंऽशुमानिव ॥३०॥

सिद्धासने स्थितो योगी मुद्रां सन्धाय वैष्णवीम् ।
शृणुयाद्दक्षिणे कर्णे नादमन्तर्गतं सदा ॥३१॥

अभ्यस्यमानो नादो यं ब्राह्ममावृणुते ध्वनिः ।
पक्षाद्विपक्षमखिलं जित्वा तुर्यपदं व्रजेत् ॥३२॥

श्रूयते प्रथमाभ्यासे नादो नानाविधो महान् ।
वर्धमाने तथाभ्यासे श्रूयते सूक्ष्मसूक्ष्मतः ॥३३॥

आदौ जलधिजीमूतभेरीनिर्झरसंभवः ।
मध्ये मर्दलशब्दाभो घण्टाकाहलजस्तथा ॥३४॥

अन्ते तु किंकिणीवंशवीणाभ्रमरनिः स्वनः ।
इति नानाविधा नादाः श्रूयन्ते सूक्ष्मसूक्ष्मतः ॥३५॥

महति श्रूयमाणे तु महाभेर्यादिकध्वनौ ।
तत्र सूक्ष्मं सूक्ष्मतरं नादमेव परामृशेत् ॥३६॥

घनमुत्सृज्य वा सूक्ष्मे सूक्ष्ममुत्सृज्य वा घने ।
रममाणमपि क्षिप्रं मनो नान्यत्र चालयेत् ॥३७॥

यत्र कुत्रापि वा नादे लगति प्रथमं मनः ।
तत्र तत्र स्थिरीभूत्वा तेन सार्धं विलीयते ॥३८॥

विस्मृत्य सकलं बाह्यं नादे दुग्धाम्बुवन्मनः ।
एकीभूयाथ सहसा चिदाकाशे विलीयते ॥३९॥

उदासीनस्ततो भूत्वा सदाभ्यासेन संयमी ।
उन्मनीकारकं सद्यो नादमेवावधारयेत् ॥४०॥

सर्वचिन्तां समुत्सृज्य सर्वचेष्टाविवर्जितः ।
नादमेवानुसंदध्यान्नादे चित्तं विलीयते ॥४१॥

मकरन्दं पिबन्भृङ्गो गन्धान्नापेक्षते यथा ।
नादासक्तं सदा चित्तं विषयं न हि कांक्षति ॥४२॥

बद्धः सुनादगन्धेन सद्यः संत्यक्तचापलः ।
नादग्रहणतश्चित्तमन्तरङ्गभुजङ्गमः ॥४३॥

विस्मृत्यं विश्वमेकाग्रः कुत्रचिन्न हि धावति ।
मनोमत्तगजेन्द्रस्य विषयोद्यानचारिणः ॥४४॥

नियामनसमर्थोऽयं निनादो निशिताङ्कुशः ।
नादोऽन्तरङ्गसारङ्गबन्धने वागुरायते ॥४५॥

अन्तरङ्गसमुद्रस्य रोधे वेलायतेऽपि वा ।
ब्रह्मप्रणवसंलग्ननादो ज्योतिर्मयात्मकः ॥४६॥

मनस्तत्र लयं याति तद्विष्णोः परमं पदम् ।
तावदाकाशसङ्कल्पो यावच्छब्दः प्रवर्तते ॥४७॥

निःशब्दं तत्परं ब्रह्म परमात्मा समीयते ।
नादो यावन्मनस्तावन्नादान्तेऽपि मनोन्मनी ॥४८॥

सशब्दश्चाक्षरे क्षीणे निःशब्दं परमं पदम् ।
सदा नादानुसंधानात्संक्षीणा वासना तु या ॥४९॥

निरञ्जने विलीयेते मनोवायू न संशयः ।
नादकोटिसहस्त्रोणि बिन्दुकोटिशतानि च ॥५०॥

सर्वे तत्र लयं यान्ति ब्रह्मप्रणवनादके ।
सर्वावस्थाविनिर्मुक्तः सर्वचिन्ताविवर्जितः ॥५१॥

मृतवत्तिष्ठते योगी स मुक्तो नात्र संशयः ।
शङ्खदुन्दुभिनादं च न शृणोति कदाचन ॥५२॥

काष्ठवज्जायते देह उन्मन्यावस्थया ध्रुवम् ।
न जानाति स शीतोष्णं न दुःखं न सुखं तथा ॥५३॥

न मानं नावमानं च सन्त्यक्त्वा तु समाधिना ।
अवस्थात्रयमन्वेति न चित्तं योगिनः सदा ॥५४॥

जाग्रन्निद्राविनिर्मुक्तः स्वरूपावस्थतामियात् ॥५५॥

दृष्टिः स्थिरा यस्य विनासदृश्यं
वायुः स्थिरो यस्य विनाप्रयत्नम् ।
चित्तं स्थिरं यस्य विनावलम्बं
स ब्रह्मतारान्तरनादरूप इत्युपनिषत् ॥५६॥

ॐ वाङ्मे मनसीति शान्तिः ।
इति नादबिन्दूपनिषत्समाप्ता ॥

NADA-BINDU UPANISHAD OF RIGVEDA

The syllable A is considered to be its (the bird Om's) right wing, U, Its left; M, its tail; and the Ardhamatra **(half-metre)** is said to be its head.

The (Rajasic and Tamasic) qualities, its feet upwards (to the loin) Sattva; its (main) body; Dharma is considered to be its right eye, and Adharma, its left.

The Bhuloka is situated in its feet; the Bhuvarloka, in its knees; the Suvarloka, in its loins; and the Maharloka, in its navel.

In its heart is situated the Janoloka; the Tapoloka in its throat, and the Satyaloka in the centre of the forehead between the eyebrows.

Then comes the Matra (or Mantra) beyond the Sahasrara (thousand-rayed).

An adept in Yoga who bestrides the Hamsa (bird) thus (viz., contemplates on Om) is not affected by Karmic influences or by tens of crores of sins.

The first Matra has Agni as the Devata (presiding deity); the second, Vayu as its Devata; the next Matra is resplendent like the sphere of the sun and the last, the Ardhamatra, the wise know as belonging to Varuna (the presiding deity of water).

Each of these Matras has indeed three Kalas (parts). This is called Omkara. Know it by means of the Dharanas, viz., concentration on each of the twelve Kalas, or the variations of the Matras produced by the difference of Svaras (or intonation). The first Matra is called Goshini; the second, Vidyunmali (or Vidyunmatra); the third, Patangini; the fourth, Vayuvegini; the fifth, Namadheya; the sixth, Aindri; the seventh, Vaishnavi; the eighth, Sankari; the ninth, Mahati; the tenth, Dhriti; the eleventh, Nari, and the twelfth Brahmi.

If a person happens to die in the first Matra (while contemplating on it), he is born again as a great emperor of Bharatavarsha.

If in the second Matra, he becomes an illustrious Yaksha; if in the third Matra, a Vidyadhara; if in the fourth, a Gandharva (these three being the celestial hosts).

If he happens to die in the fith, viz., Ardhamatra, he lives in the world of the moon, with the rank of a Deva greatly glorified there.

If in the sixth, he merges into Indra; if in the seventh, he reaches the seat of Vishnu; if in the eighth, Rudra, the Lord of all creatures.

If in the ninth, in Maharloka; if in the tenth, in Janoloka; if in the eleventh, Tapoloka; and if in the twelfth, he attains the eternal state of Brahma.

That which is beyond these, viz., Parabrahman which is beyond (above Matras) the pure, the all-pervading, beyond Kalas, the ever resplendent and the source of all Jyotis (light) should be known.

When the mind goes beyond the organs and the Gupta and is absorbed, having no separate existence and no mental action, then (the Guru) should instruct him (as to his further course of development).

That person always engaged in the contemplation and always absorbed in it should gradually leave off his body (or family) following the course of Yoga and avoiding all intercourse with society.

Then he, being freed from the bonds of Karma and the existence as a Jiva and being pure, enjoys the supreme bliss by his attaining the state of Brahman.

O intelligent man, spend your life always in the knowing of the supreme bliss, enjoying the whole of your Prarabdha (that portion of past Karma now being enjoyed) without making any complaint (of it).

Even after Atmajnana (knowledge of Atman or Self) has awakened (in one), Prarabdha does not leave(him); but he does not feel Prarabdha after the dawning of Tattva-jnana (knowledge of Tattva or truth) because the body and other things are Asat (unreal), like the things seen in a dream to one on awaking from it.

That (portion of the) Karma which is done in former births, and called Prarabdha does not at all affect the person (Tattvajnani), as there is no rebirth to him.

As the body that exists in the dreaming state is untrue, so is this body. Where then is rebirth to a thing that is illusory? How can a thing have any existence, when there is no birth (to it)?

As the clay is the material cause of the pot, so one learns from Vedanta that Ajnana is the meterial cause of the universe; and when Ajnana ceases to exist, where then is the cosmos?

As a person through illusion mistakes a rope for a serpent, so the fool not knowing Satya (the eternal Truth) sees the world (to be true).

When he knows it to be a piece of rope, the illusory idea of a serpent vanishes.

So when he knows the eternal substratum of everything and all the universe becomes (therefore) void (to him), where then is Prarabdha to him, the body being a part of the world? Therefore the word Prarabdha is accepted to enlighten the ignorant (only).

Then as Prarabdha has, in course of time, worn out, he who is the sound resulting from the union of Pranava with Brahman, who is the absolute effulgence itself, and who is the bestower of all good, shines himself like the sun at the dispersion of the clouds.

The Yogin being in the Siddhasana (posture) and practising the Vaishnavimudra, should always hear the internal sound through the right ear.

In the beginnning of his practice, he hears many loud sounds. They gradually increase in pitch and are heard more and more subtly.

At first, the sounds are like those proceeding from the ocean, clouds, kettle-drum and cataracts; in the middle (stage) those proceeding from Mardala (a musical instrument), bell, and horn.

At the last stage, those proceeding from tinkling bells, flute, Vina (a musical instrument), and bees. Thus he hears many such sounds more and more subtle.

When he comes to that stage when the sound of the great kettle-drum is being heard, he should try to distinguish only sounds more and more subtle.

He may change his concentration from the gross sound to the subtle, or from the subtle to the gross, but he should not allow his mind to be diverted from them towards others.

The mind having at first concentrated itself on any one sound, fixes firmly to that and is absorbed in it.

If (the mind) becoming insensible to the external impressions, becomes one with the sound as milk with water, and then becomes rapidly absorbed in Chidakasa (the Akasa where Chit prevails).

Being indifferent towards all objects, the Yogin having controlled his passions, should by continual practice concentrate his attention upon the sound which destroys the mind.

Having abandoned all thoughts and being freed from all actions, he should always concentrate his attention on the sound, and (then) his Chitta becomes absorbed in it.

Just as the bee drinking honey (alone) does not care for the colour, so the Chitta which is always absorbed in sound, does not long for sensual objects, as it is bound by the sweet smell of Nada and has abandoned its flitting nature.

The serpent Chitta, through listening to the Nada is entirely absorbed in it, and becoming unconscious of everything concentrates itself on the sound.

The sound serves the purpose of a sharp goad to control the maddened elephant—Chitta which roves in the pleassure-garden of the sensual objects.

It serves the purpose of a snare for binding the deer Chitta. It also serves the purpose of a shore to the ocean-waves of Chitta.

The sound proceeding from Pranava which is Brahman, is of the nature of effulgence, the mind becomes absorbed in it; that is the supreme seat of Vishnu.

The sound exists till there is the Akasic conception (Akasasankalpa). Beyond this is the (Asabda) soundless Parabrahman which is Paramatman.

The mind exists so long as there is sound, but with its (sound's) cessation, there is the state called Unmani of Manas (viz., the state of being above the mind).

The sound is absorbed in the Akshara (indestructible) and the soundless state is the supreme seat.

The mind which along with Prana (Vayu) has (its) Karmic affinites destroyed by the constant concentration upon Nada is absorbed in the unstained One. There is no doubt of it.

Many Myriads of Nadas and many more of bindus—(all) become absorbed in the Brahma-Pranava sound.

Being freed from all states and all thoughts whatever, the Yogin remains like one dead. He is a Mukta. There is no doubt about this.

After that, he does not at any time hear the sounds of conch or Dundubhi (large kettle-drum).

The body in the state of Unmani is certainly like a log and does not feel heat or cold, joy or sorrow.

The Yogin's Chitta having given up fame or disgrace is in Samadhi, above the three states.

Being freed from the waking and the sleeping states, he attains to his true state.

When the (spiritual) sight becomes fixed without any object to be seen, when the Vayu (Prana) becomes still without any effort and when the Chitta becomes firm without any support, he becomes of the form of the internal sound of Brahma-Pranava.

Such is the Upanishad.

TYAGARAJA ON NADOPASANA

Highly interesting and most popular among the forms of Nadopasana, is Sangeeta (Music). It is in Sangeeta or Sankirtana that Sreyas and Preyas otherwise antagonistic to each other meet. Sreyas is that which leads to the Eternal Good of man, viz., Self-realisation. Preyas is that which is immediately pleasant. It is generally recognised that what is Preyas is not Sreyas and vice versa. But here in Sangeeta or Sankirtana, Sreyas and Preyas are found together. Sangeeta pleases the ear, is a rich treat to the senses and the mind—in fact, so much so that the senses and the mind are tamed and controlled by it; and Sangeeta ennobles the soul and reveals the Self within. Music is, therefore, regarded as the best form of Nadopasana.

That prince among musicians, the emperor among composers, the crest-jewel among saints, the Bhakta-Siromani who adored the Lord with sweet, soul-stirring and perfect music—Sri Tyagaraja whose inspiring songs in praise of Lord Rama and on the fundamental truths of spiritual life, are sung throughout India by every lover of music for inspiration and entertainment, has repeatedly pointed out the divine glory of music. He has again and again stressed the fact that music is not food for the senses alone, but is food for the soul.

Tyagaraja says in the Kriti 'Nadopasana': "It is through Nadopasana that the Trimurtis, the sage-authors of the great scriptures, the Maharshis who have propounded Dharma, the seers who are masters of the arts and sciences, and those who are devoted to music with its three integral parts of Bhava, Raga and Tala—all these are experts in Nadopasana." It is a great truth worth remembering that all our great scriptures—Vedas, Smritis, Puranas, etc., are all set to music and are metrical compositions. There is rhythm, metre and melody in them. Sama Veda, especially, is unrivalled in its music. That is why Sri Tyagaraja regards all the Maharshis and seers as Nadopasakas.

Tyagaraja says: "The knowledge of the science of music is capable of bestowing on you the State of Sarupya" (in his Kriti 'Sngeeta Sastra Jnanamu'). Why? Because "All sounds have emanated from Om" (In his Kriti 'Nadasudha'). He continues: "This nectar (Sangeeta) which is the essence of Pranava—the Omkara which is itself the essence of all Vadas, Agamas, Sastras and Puranas—can remove all your miseries and bestow eternal bliss upon you." He crowns this declaration with the marvellous revelation: "It is this Sangeeta that has taken form in this word as Rama." That is why he said in another Kriti that he who adores the Lord through Sangeeta will attain Sarupya Mukti. For, Sangeeta is identical with God; and in accordance with the truth you become what you intently mediate upon, the Nadopasaka becomes Nada-svarupa or God.

Sangeeta is not mere nerve-titillation. It is a Yoga. Emphasising this truth, Sri Tyagaraja says in his 'Sripapriya': "Music which is composed of the seven Svaras is a treasure for the great Tapasvins who have cooled the Taapa-Traya (Adhyatmika, Adhidaivika and Adhibhoutika Taapas)."

In fact, Tyagaraja would go for as to declare that Moksha is impossible for one who has no music in him! He says in 'Mokshamudgara': "Is there Moksha for those who have no knowledge of music which is based on Bhakti, who do not realise the truth that the Sapta-Svaras have emanated from the Pranava which is born of the union of Prana and Agni, and who have a liking for the mere melody of the Vina, but have not understood the Siva-Tattva?" Thus, whilst music is exalted to the status of a potent Sadhana for Moksha, Tyagaraja does not fail always to point out that the mere utterance of sounds will not bestow Moksha upon the songster and that the realisation of the Source and Goal of Music ought to be sought after.

If one realises this Truth, he attains Jivanmukti. Tyagaraja says in his 'Ragasudharasa': "Drink the nectar of Raga and get enlightened. Whatever Siddhi, the most difficult practices like Yaga, Yoga, etc., can bestow on you, you will easily get through Nadopasana. They are Jivanmuktas who have ralised that Music which is nothing but Omkara born of the Self and which has Nada for its body—this Music adorned by the Sapta-Svaras is itself the Form of Sadasiva." Therefore it is that the Sadhaka is exhorted to realise the Siva-Tattva which is the Substratum for music.

One cannot but be deeply moved at the wonderful tribute that Tyagaraja pays to Music, the Nadopasana, in his song; 'Intakanna-anandamemi' in which he says: "Singing Thy glorious Names in melodious tunes and dancing in joy with the sole aim of having Thy Darshan—will this not do? Is this not the state for which even sages aspire?" For Tyagaraja declares, Nadopasana itself bestows Advaitic realisation on the Sadhaka. He says in the same song: "In Thee I perceive the world and I merge myself in Thee, with my intellect clear and illumined."

May you all realise the Self through Nadopasana.

MUSICO-THERAPY

Music is Sabda Brahman.
Mark the power of gentle, sweet sounds.
Sa, ri, ga, ma, pa, dha, ni, sa.
Music has charms to soothe a ferocious tiger.
It melts rocks and bends the banyan tree.
It enraptures, lulls and energises.
It elevates, inspires, strengthens and invigorates.
It vibrates in the memory.
It cures incurable diseases.
There is music in the running brooks.
There is music in the cry of children.
There is music in all things, if you have ears.
Man wants music to relax and elevate him.
The devotee sits with his Ekatara, Tambura,
To melt his mind in his Lord in silence.
Narada Rishi roams about in the three worlds,
With his Tambura in his hand, singing,
"Sriman Narayana, Narayana, Narayana."
Music helps the devotee to commune with the Lord.
It makes the mind one-pointed quickly.
Anahta music steadies the mind.
Hear it daily and melt the mind in silence.
Practise Yoni Mudra to hear the Anahata.
Enter into Samadhi through steady practice.

Music is Nada Brahman. Sama Veda is full of high class music. Ravana chanted Sama Veda and propitiated Lord Siva.

Bhava, Raga and Tala—these three constitute the whole conception of Nada Laya which leads to Nada Brahman.

Gita, Vadya and Nritya—these three make up Sangita which is offered in the service of the Lord.

Music captivates the mind. Music elevates the mind to sublime heights of divine splendour. Music causes Laya or dissolution of the mind in Brahman or the Absolute.

Harmonium, Vina, Sitar, Sarangi, Dilroba, Violin, Villu, Yal, Swaramandal, Harp, etc., are the various kinds of musical instruments which express the various times that help the Laya process.

Music is an aid in the treatment of diseases. Music has an extrordinary power over diseases. Harmonious rhythm caused by sweet music has attractive property. It draws out disease. The disease comes out to encounter the music wave. The two blend together and vanish in space.

Music soothes the brain and the nerves. It lulls the whole system. It stimulates, energises, invigorates, galvanises and vitalises the whole system. It affects the emotions and arouses the impulses to action and thereby influences all the vital functions. It consists of a series of harmonious vibrations, electrical in their nature and make up.

Music relaxes nervous tension and makes those parts of the body affected by tension to resume their normal functions.

Music is highly beneficial in the treatment of nervous disorders, sleeplessness, etc.

Music has tremendous power to bring comfort and solace when one is in a state of despondency or pain.

Book Three

KRIYA YOGA

KRIYA YOGA

तप: स्वाध्यायेश्वरप्रणिधानानि क्रियायोग: ।

Austerities, study of scriptures and self-surrender constitute the Yoga of Purificatoty Action.

TAPAS

कायेन्द्रियसिद्धिरशुद्धिक्षयात्तपस: ।

Through Tapas, mortification, due to the destruction of impurities, arise psychic powers in the body and senses.

By Tapas, the mind, speech and Indriyas are purified. Fasts and all religious observances that are laid down in Dharma Sastras and the rules of Yama and Niyama, Asana, Pranayama, etc., come under Tapas. In Gita Chapter XVII, the three Slokas from 14 to 16 describe three kinds of Tapas, viz., Tapas of body, speech and mind. Psychic powers are the eight Siddhis, Anima, Mahima, etc. All these Siddhis can be acquired by the steady practice of Tapas. Manu says: "He whose speech and mind are pure and ever carefully guarded, obtains all the fruits that are obtained by means of Vedanta." By the performance of Tapas, all Klesas (afflictions) and impurities can be destroyed.

WHAT IS TAPAS?

That which purifies the impure mind is Tapas. That which regenerates the lower animal nature and generates divine nature is Tapas. That which cleanses the mind and destroys lust, anger, greed, etc., is Tapas. That which produces Brahma-Tejas and destroys Asuric or diabolical nature is Tapas. That which destroys Tamas and Rajas and increases Sattva is Tapas. That which steadies the mind, and fixes it on the Eternal is Tapas. That which arrests the outgoing tendencies, extroversion or Bahirmukhi Vritti and produces introversion or Antarmukha Vritti is Tapas. That which destroys Vasanas, egoism, Raga-Dvesha and generates dispassion, discrimination and meditation is Tapas. Tapas is spiritual discipline, Yogabhyasa or Brahmabhyasa. Tapas is Brahma-Chintana, worship, Sadhana and meditation.

This is the third Anga of Niyama in Raja Yoga. It is one of the three items of Kriya Yoga. Tapas means austerity or practice of penance. The man of Tapas is brilliant like a blazing fire. Tapas means restraint of the senses and meditation also. Tapas leads to control of mind.

Standing on one leg, raising one hand up for a long time is also Tapas. But this is Tamasic Tapas of an ignorant man. Panchagni Tapas is sitting in the midst of four fires in the hot sun, having sun as the fifth fire. Vairagis practise this very often. Desire moves the senses. Desire can be controlled only if the senses are curbed. Tapas annihilates desires. Practise intelligent Tapas.

Tapas is austerity, control of senses and meditation. The aspirant is blazing like fire (Tapati). His eyes are brilliant, his voice sweet and forcible. His body is shining and beautiful. All are attracted towards him. He is like a magnet. All these are due to his Tapascharya. He who does Tapas is Tapasvin. Tapasvin go to Tapoloka. Brahma did Tapas (meditation) before he created the universe. He reflected over his grand plan of creation. This is his Tapas. Purify yourself through Tapas and attain the ultimate goaL

FORMS OF TAPAS

Standing in water in winter is a lower form of Tapas. Standing in hot sun in summer is another lower form of Tapas. Panchagni Tapas is another form of Tapas. Living on sweet neem-leaves or dried leaves is another type of Tapas. Perambulating round Govardhana hill with Namaskara is another form of Tapas. Tratak on the sun, walking barefooted, living naked in snowy regions, fasting and Vratas like Chandrayana Vrata, Ekadasi Vrata, Pradosha Vrata, Kriscchra Vrata, Mouna or vow of silence, Anushthana, Purascharana, vigils etc., are different kinds of Tapas.

THREE KINDS OF TAPAS

Tapas is of three kinds viz., physical, verbal and mental. Brahmacharya, service of Guru and saints, practice of Ahimsa or non-violence are all Tapas of the body. Through the power of Brahmacharya Bhishma and Hunuman did marvellous deeds. Through the power of Chastity, Damayanti burnt the hunter, Anasuya converted the Trimurtis into babies, Savitri brought back Satyavan from Lord Yama. The power of Brahmacharya is more powerfil than the power of physical Tapas. To speak the truth, to observe vow of silence, not to hurt others by unkind words or harsh words, to speak words that are beneficial, study of scriptures are all Tapas of the speech. Poise, mental restraint or Shama, purity of nature, one-pointedness of mind, mental happines, cheerfulness, cleanliness of life, are all Tapas of mind.

ABANDON TAPAS-ABHIMANA

Visvamitra's Tapas was of a Rajasic type. He had Tapas-Abhimana. He was egoistic and was proud of his Tapas. He always fought with the Sattvic Vasishtha. His pride was quelled in the end. Both went to Lord Brahma, the creator, to find out "Who is a greater Tapasvin?" Brahma said, "He who brings the Surya Devata in my presence is a great Tapasvin." Visvamitra approached Surya. Surya said, "Bring somebody to take up my work. I shall come to Brahma now." Visvamitra was not able to do it. Thereupon Vasishtha placed his Brahma Danda. It shone with brilliance and did the work of Sun. Surya came to Brahma and paid his respects. Visvamitra put his head down in shame and silently repaired to his abode. Therefore abandon Tapas-Abhimana. Practise Sattvic Tapas and give up Tamasic Tapas. Make the Tapas Sattvic and destroy egoism through self-surrender or Atma Bhava.

MENTAL TAPAS

Mental Tapas is more powerful than physical Tapas. He who bears heat and cold does physical Tapas. He increases his power of endurance, but he may not be able to bear insult. He will be easily upset by a harsh or unkind word. He may take revenge and do tit for tat. He has no control over the mind. He has disciplined only his physical body. To keep a balanced mind in all conditions of life, to bear insult, injury and persecutions, to be ever serene, contented and peaceful, to be cheerful in adverse conditions, to have fortitude in meeting danger, to have presence of mind and forbearance are all forms of mental Tapas.

HIGHEST TAPAS

Conventionally, eating neem-leaves, standing in water, sitting in the hot sun, bearing heat and cold, standing on one leg with raised hands, etc., are considered as Tapas. People speak of such persons as Tapasvins. They say, "Ram Brahmachari is a great Tapasvin. He lives on leaves and has no clothing. He does Panchagni Tapas in hot summer." These are all forms of physical Tapas. Fixing the wandering mind on God or Brahman is great Tapas. Vichara and Nididhyasana are the highest Tapas. Enquiry of 'who am I?' is the supreme Tapas. Pratyahara, Pranayama, Dharana and Samadhi, practice of the four means, Navavidha Bhakti are great Tapas.

SVADHYAYA.

स्वाध्यायादिष्टदेवतासंप्रयोगः

By study of scriptures comes the communion with the tutelary deity.

Svadhyaya is the study of scriptures such as Gita, Upanishads, Ramayana, Bhagavata, etc. The study should be done with concentration. You should understand what you have studied and try to put in your everyday life all that you have learnt. There will be no benefit in your study if you do not exert to live up to the teachings of the scriptures. Svadhyaya includes also

Japa, the repetition of Mantras. Constant study and its practice in daily life will lead one to have communion with God.

ISVARAPRANIDHANA

समाधिसिद्धिरीश्वरप्रणिधानात् ।

By self-surrender comes the attainment of Samadhi, superconscious state.

The self-surrender should be free, perfect, unconditioned and ungrudging. Then the Samadhi will come by itself. This Isvarapranidhana is highest self-surrender.

Atma Nivedana is self-surrender. In the Vishnu Sahasranama it is said: "The heart of one who has taken refuge in Vasudeva, who is wholly devoted to Vasudeva, gets entirely purified, and he attains Brahman, the Eternal."

The devotee offers everything to God including his body, mind and soul. He keeps nothing for himself. He loses even his own little self. He has no personal and independent existence. He has given up his self for God. He has become part and parcel of God. God takes care of him and God treats him as Himself. Grief and sorrow, pleasure and pain, the devotee treats as gifts sent by God and does not attach himself to them. He considers himself as a puppet of God and an instrument in the hands of God. He does not feel egoistic, for he has no ego. His ego has gone over to God. It is not his duty to take care of his wife, children, etc., for he himself has no independent existence apart from God. God will take care of all. He knows how to lead the world in the right path. One need not think that he is born to lead the world. God is there who will look to everything which man cannot even dream of. He has no sensual craving for he has no body as it is offered to God. He does not adore or love his body for it is God's business to see to it. He only feels the presence of God and nothing else. He is fearless for God is helping him at all times. He has no enemy for he has given himself up to God who has no enemies or friends. He has no anxiety for he has attained everything by attaining the grace of God. He has not even the thought of salvation; rather he does not want salvation, even, he merely wants God and nothing but God. He is satisfied with the love of God, for by that there is nothing that is not attained. What is there to be attained when God has sent His Grace upon the devotee? The devotee does not want to become sugar but taste sugar. There is pleasure in tasting sugar, but not in becoming sugar itself. So the devotee feels that there is supreme joy more in loving God than in becoming God. God shall take complete care of the devotee. 'I am Thine' says the devotee.

This self-surrender is Absolute Love for God alone. There is nothing but God-consciousness in the devotee. Even against his own wishes, the devotee shall become one with God and lose his individuality. This is the law of being. The Highest Truth is Absoluteness and the soul rises above through different states of consciousness until it attains Absolute perfection when it becomes identical with God. This is the culmination of all aspiration and love.

There are innumerable verses in the Bhagavadgita and the Bhagavata establishing the truth that self-surrender is the only way to attain the Supreme.

Krishna teaches to Arjuna that self-surrender, total and exclusive, alone can give him peace and relieve him from all sins.

One who studies the Bhagavadgita and the Srimad Bhagavata will come to know what a great importance is given to total self-surrender. For self-surrender is the annihilation of individual consciousness and the attainment of Absoslute Consciousness. This is equal to Nirvikalpa Samadhi.

The devotee flies to the state of the highest Mahabhava and merges himself in God. The wave subsides in the ocean. The spark becomes one with fire.The ray is absorbed into the Sun. The mind merges in the Atman.The individual loses itself in the Absolute. The devotee becomes one with God. Worldly consciousness vanishes into universal consciousness. Man becomes God and the mortal becomes Immortal.

SECRET OF SURRENDER

Sakrideva prapannaya tavasmiti cha yachate
Abhayam sarvabhutebhyo dadamyetad vritam mama.

"I remove all fears of all beings even if they come to Me only once and seek My refuge; calling themselves as Mine—This is my vow." *(Sri Ramachandra's vow)*

Throughout the Gita there is a ringing note that surrender and devotion are absolutely necessary for the attainment of God-consciousness. In reality, the nine modes of devotion (Navavidha Bhakti) are reducible to one, viz., Atmanivedana. The following Gita slokas will impress on your mind the importance of devotion and self-surrender.

Tameva saranam gaccha sarvabhavena bharata
Tatprasadat param santim sthanam prapsyasi
sasvatam

"Flee unto Him for shelter with all thy being. O Bharata; by His grace thou shalt obtain supreme peace, the everlasting dwelling-peace."(XVIII. 62)

Manmana bhava madbhakto madyajee man
namaskuru
Mamevaishyasi satyam te pratijane priyosi me.

"Merge thy mind in Me, be My devotee, sacrifice to Me, prostrate thyself before Me, thou shalt come even to Me." (XVIII. 65)

Sarvadharman parityajya mamekam saranam vraja
Aham tva sarvapapebhyo mokshayishyami ma suchah.

"Abandoning all duties come to Me, for shelter; sorrow not, I liberate thee from all sins."(XVIII. 66)

Slokas 65 and 66 of Chapter XVIII are the most important Slokas of the Gita. The gist of the teachings of Lord Krishna is here. If anyone can live in the true spirit of these Slokas, he will realise the goal of life soon. There is no doubt of this.

The self-surrender must be total ungrudging and unreserved. You must not keep certain desires for gratification. Mira says: "I have given my whole heart, mind, intellect, soul, my all to my Giridhara Gopala." This is perfect self-surrender.

A real devotee will not ask the Lord even for Mukti. So long as the subtle desire for liberation lingers in one's heart he cannot claim himself to be a true devotee of the Lord. Though the desire for emanicapation is of Sattivic nature, yet the devotee has become a slave of Mukti. He is still selfish and so is unfit to call himself a sincere lover of God. He has not yet made total, unreserved self-surrender. To ask for Mukti is a variety of hypocrisy. Can true devotee dare ask anything from God, when he fully knows that He is an ocean of love and compassion?

A real devotee never complains against God. A raw Bhakta speaks ill of God when he is in distress. He says "I have done 25 lakhs of Japa. I am studying Bhagavata daily. Yet God is not pleased with me. He has not removed my suffering. God is blind.He has not heard my prayers. What sort of God is Lord Krishna? I have no faith in Him."

A real Bhakta rejoices in suffering, pain and destitution. He welcomes grief and sorrow always so that he may not forget God even for a second. He has the firm belief that God does everything for his good only. Kunti Devi prayed to Krishna: "O Lord! give me pain always. Then only I will remember Thee always."

In Puri a saint who completely dedicated himself to Lord Hari was seriously ailing from chronic dysentery. He became quite helpless. Lord Hari of Puri was serving him for months in the form of a servant. The Law of Prarabdha is inexorable. Nobody can escape from the operation of this infallible law. The Lord did not want the Bhakta to take another birth for the exhaustion of his Prarabdha. So His devotee has to suffer from protracted ailment. This was his Karmic purgation. But He Himself served him, as the devotee surrended himself completely. Look at the unbounded mercy of the Lord. He becomes a slave of His devotees when they entirely depend upon Him.

Self-surrender does not mean retirement into the forests. It does not mean giving up of all activities. Tamas or inertia is mistaken for self-surrender. This is a sad mistake. What is wanted is internal surrender. The ego and desire must be annihilated. This will constitute real surrender. The Rajasic mind stands obstinate to effect complete self-surrender. Obstinacy is a great obstacle to surrender. The lower nature again and again rises up to assert itself. There is resurrection of desires. Desires get suppressed for some time. Again they manifest themselves with redoubled force. Man is dragged hither and thither by these desires. Believe in the Divine possibilities. Completely dedicate yourself to the Lord. Have full trust in Him. Rest in peace. All cares, worries, anxieties, tribulations and egoistic efforts will terminate now.

Look at Prahlada's surrender and faith in God! He completely resigned himself to Lord Hari. No other thought save thoughts of God occupied his mind. He had His full Grace and benediction even though he was ill-treated by his father in a variety of ways. He was hurled down from the top of a cliff. He was trampled upon by the elephant. He was poisoned. He was thrown into the sea with the legs tied by iron-chains. Cobras were thrown over him. His nose was filled with poisonous gas. He was thrown into fire. Boiling oil was poured over his head. Yet his faith in Narayana was not shaken even a bit. The name of Narayana was always on his lips. Such must be the faith of every devotee.

Pray to God fervently: "O Lord! Make my will strong to resist all temptations, to control my Indriyas and lower nature, to change my old evil habits and to make my surrender complete and real. Enthrone Thyself in my heart. Do not leave this place even for a second. Use my body, mind and organs as Thy instruments. Make me fit to dwell in Thee for ever."

Give up all ideas of duty and responsibility. Allow the Divine Will to work unhampered now. This is the secret of surrender. You will feel you are a changed being. This exalted state is ineffable. A great transformation will come upon you. You will be enveloped by a halo of divine effulgence. You will be drowned in indescribable bliss, peace and joy. Your old little self is dead now. You are now a changed spiritual being. Your individual will is merged in the Cosmic Will. You are now illumined by the Divine Light. All ignorance has melted now. Enjoy the immortal divine life wherein there is neither despair nor fear, neither hunger nor thirst, neither doubt nor delusion. Shine in Divine Splendour and Glory.

SELF-SURRENDER

Self-surrender is Saranagati or Atmanivedana. This is one of the nine modes of Bhakti. The Bhakta (devotee) starts with Sravana or hearing the Lilas and Gunas of the Lord, slowly ascends the different rungs in the ladder of Bhakti Yoga and ultimately reaches the highest rung, Atmanivedana. The will of the devotee becomes one with the Cosmic Will. The devotee becomes one with the Lord and enjoys all divine Aisvaryas (Vibhutis). Eight Siddhis and nine Riddhis roll under his feet. They stand with folded hands to obey implicitly the commands of the devotee. The devotee feels and sees the Lord in every hair follicle of his body, in every atom and molecule. This state is Achintya (unthinkable) and Anirdesya (indescribable). Lord speaks and works through the different organs of His Bhakta, as his egoism is totally destroyed. The obstacles that stand in the way of self-surrender are desires and egoism. The self-surrender must be total, unreserved, ungrudging and unconditioned. Sometimes the devotee keeps certain desires for his own gratification. That is the reason why he is not able to make perfect self-surrender and have Darsana of his Ishta. The egoism is very stiff and obstinate. It is like hard granite. It has to be split asunder through constant hammering with the chisel of Bhakti. Even the very hard diamond is pierced through by another harder material and a slender wire is passed through the hole in the diamond when a necklace is made. Even so this hard Antahkarana or heart must be pierced through by self-surrender and the slender thread of Bhakti must be passed through the heart. Then only the Lord will take His seat in the heart of His devotee.

The devotee even expects God to do the self-surrender for himself. This is mere foolishness only. He will have to do the self-surrender himself. Remember this point well.

Tamas or inertia is mistaken for self-surrender. In Patanjali Yoga Sutras there is an aphorism *Isvarapranidhanadva*—"Samadhi can be attained by surrendering the little self and the fruits of one's actions at the feet of the Lord." Self-surrender is one of the three limbs of Kriya Yoga. Then again self-surrender is one of the five items in Niyama. The Kriya Yoga destroys the five Klesas (afflictions) and prepares the mind for union with the Lord.

Lord Krishna says in the Gita: "Abandoning all duties, come unto Me alone for shelter, sorrow not. I will liberate thee from sins." This is a powerful Saranagati-mantra that will help the devotee in effecting his self-surrender if he keeps up the Bhava of this Sloka constantly before his mind.

This corresponds to the Saranagati-mantra '*Sri Ramah Saranam Mama*—I surrender myself to Sri Rama' of Bhaktas of Sri Rama, '*Sri Krishna Saranam Mama*—I surrender myself to Sri Krishna' of Bhaktas of Lord Krishna, '*Sriman-Narayanacharanau Saranam Prapadye*—I surrender myself to Lord Narayana' of Bhaktas of Lord Hari. Those who repeat the above Mantras with Bhava will get the grace of the Lord soon. They will be able to do perfect self-surrender.

Repetition of these formulae, "I am Thine, my Lord, All is Thine, Thy Will be done" will help you in getting Lord's grace and in effecting self-surrender. Even if you say once from the core of your heart, from the central, inner being, with one-pointed devotion, with 100 per cent of your mind or 16 annas of mind 'I am Thine, my Lord' the gulf that separates you from God will be bridged over at once. The mind, Chitta, heart, intellect and soul should all combine harmoniously effecting the surrender. Then only the self-surrender will be true, complete and perfect. If the mind says 'I am Thine my Lord,' if the Buddhi says 'I am Mr. so and so. I am an M.L.C. I know everything. I am a powerful judge,' if Chitta says 'I must have the Siddhi to get whatever I want' and if the soul says 'I am a great devotee,' you are only a hypocrite. You have not made any kind of self-surrender. Beware of moral and spiritual pride. Maya assumes various subtle forms. Moral and spiritaul pride of aspirants are more dangerous than the ordinary pride of wealth, power and position of worldly-minded persons.

SHATKRIYAS IN HATHA YOGA

The six purificatory exercises are Dhauti, Basti, Neti, Nauli, Tratak and Kapalabhati.

DHAUTI

Purification is of two kinds, internal and external. Internal purification can be made in several ways. Here you will find the technique of an important exercise.

Take a fine piece of cloth, 3 inches wide and 15 feet long. The borders should be stitched well and no loose thread should be hanging from the sides. Wash it with soap and keep it always clean. Dip it in tepid water. Squeeze out the water and swallow one end of it little by little. On the first day swallow only one foot length of the cloth and draw it out slowly. After gradual practice you can swallow the whole length by catching one end of it. Keep it in the stomach for a few minutes and then slowly draw it out. Do not be hasty and draw out the cloth forcibly. When the Kriya is over, drink a cup of milk. This is a sort of lubrication, for the throat. Do this when the stomach is empty. Morning time is good. It will be quite sufficient if you practise this, once in 4 or 5 days. This is an excellent exercise for those who are of a flabby and phlegmatic constitution. Gradual and steady practice cures gulma, gastritis and dyspepsia and all other diseases of the stomach.

BASTI

Basti is intended to remove congestion in the intestines. There are two varieties in this exercise, viz., Sthala Basti and Jala Basti.

Sthala Basti: Sit on the ground, stretch your legs. Now catch hold of your toes with the hands. This is like Paschimottanasana, but here, you need not bend much till your head touches the knees. Catching hold of the toes with the hands, churn the abdominal muscles slowly with a downward motion. Contract sphincter muscles. After this practice, you will have a free motion.

Jala Basti: This is more effective. Sqat in a tank or river, very near the shore, where the water is not more than knee-deep. The buttocks should not touch the ground. The trunk may be slightly bent forward. Now perform Uddiyana Bandha twice or thrice and thus throw out all the air from the abdomen. Then do Nauli Kriya. Open the anus through Asvini Mudra. Now a vacuum is created within the abdomen and water automatically enters the colon. Then, come out of water and again with the help of Uddiyana Bandha and Asvini Mudra expel the water from the colon.

You can sit in a tub containing water and do this. In the initial state, you may need to insert a small bamboo tube five inches long, to help you keep the anus open. If you use the bamboo tube, then lubricate one end of it with vaseline.

This is only for occasional practice to remove accumulation in intestines.

NETI

Unclean nostrils will lead you to irregular breathing. Irregular breathing will make you sick. Neti Kriya is intended for the purification of nostrils. Take a fine piece of strong thread. There should be no knots throughout. Insert the ends of the thread into each nostril and catch hold of the loose thread firmly. By deep inhalation, you can draw the thread inside. Then slowly put it out. Do this through both nostrils. The nostrils will be thoroughly cleansed.

NAULI

Nauli is a powerful exercise for regenerating, invigorating and stimulating the abdominal viscera and the gastro-intestinal or ailmentary system. For the practice of Nauli, you should have a good practice of Uddiyana Bandha.

Stand, legs a foot apart and rest your hands on the thighs with a slight curve of the back. Do a strong and forcible expiration through the mouth and keep the lungs completely empty. Contract and forcibly draw the abdoiminal muscles towards the back. This is Uddiyana Bandha. This is the first stage of Nauli.

Then let loose the centre of the abdomen and contract the left and right side of the abdomen. You will have all the muscles in the centre in a vertical line. This is called Madhyama Nauli. Keep it as long as you can retain in the position comfortably. Then you can release the muscles and inhale. This is the second stage of Nauli.

After some practice, contract the right side of the abdomen and let loose the left side free. You will now have all the muscles on the left side only. This is called Vama Nauli. Again contract the left side and let loose the right side. This is Dakshina Nauli. By such gradual practice, you will understand how to contract the muscles of the central, left and right side of the abdominal muscles from side to side. Practise like this for a few days.

Then draw the muscles in the centre. Slowly move them to the right side and then to the left side in a circular way. Do this several times from the right to left and then do it in a reverse way from the left to right side. You should move the muscles always with a circular motion slowly. When you advance in the practice you can do it quickly. This last stage of Nauli will appear like 'churning' when the abdominal muscles are isolated and rotated from side to side. When Nauli is demonstrated by advanced students, you will be surprised to observe the movements of the abdominal muscles. It will look as if an engine is working in the abdominal factory.

When beginners want to do Dakshina Nauli, they have to slightly bend towards the left side and contract left muscles. When they want to do Vama Nauli, they have to bend a little to the right side. In Madhyama Nauli push the entire muscles forward by contracting the two sides.

Nauli Kriya eradicates chronic constipation, dyspepsia and all other diseases of the gastro-intestinal system. The liver and pancreas are toned. All other abdominal organs will function properly.

TRATAK

This is steady gazing at a particular point or object without winking. This is mainly intended for developing the power of concentration and mental focus. This is very useful for all.

Sit on Padmasana or Siddhasana. You can sit erect even on a chair. Keep the picture of your Ishta Devata or the picture of Om or a black dot on a piece of white paper. Look at the point or picture very steadily. You can gaze at a bright star or on the flames of a ghee-lamp. Gazing at the tip of the nose and at the space between the eyebrows is also Tratak. When you gaze at a particular point or picture, it is Tratak. Close your eyes and form a mental picture of the object. Practise this for 2 minutes and cautiously increase the period.

Tratak improves eye-sight. Diseases of the eyes are removed. Many have thrown away their spectacles after some practice in Tratak. It develops the power of concentration to a great degree.

KAPALABHATI

Kapalabhati is an exercise for cleansing the skull. Kapala means `skull' and Bhati means 'to shine'. This exercise makes the skull shining.

Sit on Padmasana or Siddhasana. Close the eyes. Perform Rechaka and Puraka rapidly. This should be practised vigorously. One will get perspiration profusely. This is a good exercise for the lungs also. Those who are well-versed in Kapalabhati can do Bhastrika very easily. Rechaka should be done forcibly by contracting the abdominal muscles. Do 20 expulsions for a round and gradually increase the number to 120. In Kapalabhati there is no Kumbhaka. Kapalabhati cleanses the respiratory system and the nasal passages. It removes the spasm in bronchial tubes. Consequently Asthma is relieved and also cured in course of time. The apices of the lungs get proper oxygenation. Consumption is cured. Impurities of the blood are thrown out. The circulatory and respiratory systems are toned to a considerable degree.

PRANAYAMA

Sit on Padmasana or Siddhasana. Slowly inhale the air through both the nostrils without making any sound. Do not retain the breath. Immediately exhale the air very, very slowly. Repeat this process ten or twenty times both morning and evening. Practise this regularly for three months. Then you can attempt for the Sukha Purvaka exercise where there is retention of breath.

Inhalation is termed as `Puraka'; `Rechaka' is exhalation and `Kumbhaka' is retention.

Svasa refers to Puraka and Prasvasa refers to Rechaka.

ATI-SUKHA-PURVAKA PRANAYAMA

*Technique:*Sit comfortably on a chair, sofa or easy chair. Draw the air through both nostrils, as long as comfortable. Retain as long as comfortable. Repeat your Ishta Mantra or Om retaining the breath. Then exale as long as comfortable. You need not observe any ratio between the inhalation, exhalation and retention; but let the inhalation and exhalation be deep and full.

*Benefits:*The benefits of this Pranayama are incalculable. All the muscles are relaxed. All the nerves are toned.Rhythm and harmony is established in the entire being. Mind is calmed. Circulation is promoted. An inexpressible peace and bliss come to reign within you.

You can do it in the morning while lying in bed. Your mind will become alert for commencing Japa and Dhyana. You can do it when the mind is about to lose balance on account of the setting in of lust, anger or other evil Vrittis; the mind will be filled with a great power that will prevent the evil Vrittis from disturbing it. You can do it just before commencing your study; mind will be concentrated easily and what you study will be indelibly impressed in your mind. You can do it during your office-work; you will get new strength every time and you will never be tired. When you return home from the office you can practise this Pranayama and you will be recharged with fresh energy.

The greatest advantage is that once you start doing it you will do it very often; and your mind can never find an excuse for not practising this Ati-Sukha-Purvaka Pranayama, very very easy and comfortable Pranayama which has all the advantages of Pranayama, without its 'rules and regulations'. Do it from now without fail.

SUKHA PURVAKA PRANAYAMA

Sit on Padmasana or Siddhasana in your meditation room. Close the right nostril with the right thumb. Draw in air slowly through the left nostril. Now close the left nostril also with the little and ring fingers of the right hand. Retain the breath as long as you can comfortably do. Then exhale very, very slowly through the right nostril after removing the thumb. Now half the process is over.

Then draw in the air through the right nostril as soon as you completely exhale. Retain the breath as long as you can after closing the right nostril and then exhale through the left nostril after removing the little and the ring fingers. These six processes constitute one Pranayama. To start with, do 10 Pranayams in the morning and 10 in the evening. Gradually increase the number to 20 in each sitting. Gradually increase the period of Kumbhaka also. Have a Bhava (mental attitude) that all the Daivi Sampat as mercy, love, forgiveness, Santi, Joy etc,. are entering your system along with the inspired air and all the Asuri Sampat such as lust, anger, greed etc., are being thrown out along with the exhaled air. Repeat Om or Gayatri mentally during Puraka, Kumbhaka and Rechaka. This Pranayama exercise removes all diseases, purifies the Nadis, steadies the mind in concentrtion.

The next exercise is Kevala Kumbhaka wherein is neither Puraka nor Rechaka. There is Kumbhaka only. This is Kumbhaka only. This is for advanced Yogins. Kumbhaka is of two kinds, viz., Sahita and Kevala. That which is coupled with inhalation and exhalation is termed as Sahita Kumbhaka, which is described above. That which is devoid of Puraka and Rechaka is Kevala Kumbhaka. After you get mastery over Sahita, it is said, "when after giving up of inhalation and exhalation, one holds his breath with ease, it is Kevala Kumbhaka (absolute)." He attains perfection.

BENEFITS OF PRANAYAMA

The ignorance caused by the Karma covers the light of knowledge. By the practice of Pranayama this covering is destroyed by the development of concentration and knowledge.

HINTS ON PRANAYAMA

In the early morning answer the calls of nature and then sit for the practice. Pranayama should be done in a well-ventilated room. Pranayama requires deep concentration and attention. Do not keep anyone by your side.

When you finish the practice, take a cup of milk, after 10 minutes. Do not take bath immediately.

Do not perform Pranayama till you get fatigued. In the beginning of the practice you may not be able to get the time-unit for doing Puraka, Kumbhaka and Rechaka—the ratio is 1:4:2. When you have advanced in the practice the ratio will come by itself; and you need not distract the mind in counting and keeping time-unit. Regular, steady practice is needed for a long time.

CONCENTRATION

Concentration is practised for stopping the modifications of the mind. Concentration is holding the mind to one form or object for a long time.

To remove the tossing and various other obstacles which stand in the way of one-pointedness, the practice of concentration on one thing alone should be made.

Concentration is opposed to sensuous desires, bliss to flurry and worry, sustained thinking to perplexity, applied thinking to sloth and torpor, rapture to ill-will.

There is no limit to the power of the human mind. The more concentrated it is, the more power is brought about to bear on one point.

The rays of the mind are scattered in the case of the wordly-minded persons. There is dissipation of mental energy in various directions. For the purpose of concentration, these scattered rays have to be gathered by the practice of concentration and then the mind must be made to turn towards God.

Concentration is fixing the mind on something external or internal. The mind can be fixed externally on the picture of Lord Hari, Lord Krishna or Lord Rama or any other object or point. Internally it can be fixed on any Chakra or any part of the body or on any abstract idea.

It is easy to concentrate the mind on external objects. The mind has a natural tendency to go outwards.

Keep the picture of Sri Krishna, Rama, Narayana, Devi or Lord Jesus or any picture, in front of you. Look at it steadily without winking. Gaze at the head, then at the body, then at the legs. Repeat the same process again and again. When your mind calms down look at a particular spot only. Then close the eyes and mentally visualise the picture.

You should be able to visualise the picture very clearly even in its absence. You will have to call up the mental picture at a moment's notice. Keep it there steadily for some time. This is concentration. You will have to practise this daily. If you want to increase your power of concentration, you will have to reduce your worldly desires and activities. You will have to observe silence every day for some hours. Then only the mind can concentrate very easily and without difficulty.

Sit in lotus-pose (Padmasana) with crossed legs. Fix the gaze on the tip of the nose. This is called the nasal gaze. Do not make any violent effort. Gently look at the tip of the nose. Practise for one minute in the beginning. Gradually increase the time to half an hour or more. This practice steadies the mind. It develops the power of concentration. Even when you walk you can keep up this practice.

Sit in lotus-pose and practise fixing the mind between the two eyebrows. Do this gently for half a minute. Then gradually increase the time to half an hour or more. There must not be the least violence in the practice. This removes tossing of mind and develops concentration. This is known as frontal gaze.

Practise concentration till the mind is well established on the object of concentration. When the mind runs away from the object bring it back again and again. Even if the mind runs outside during your practice, do not bother much. Allow it to run. Slowly try to bring it to your object of concentration. By repeated practice the mind will be finally focussed on your object. He who has gained abstraction (withdrawing the senses from the objects) will have good concentration.

After having gained strength in the practice of external concentration, you can concentrate internally on any of the seven Chakras (centres) of spiritual energy. Attention plays a very prominent part in concentration.

By practising concentration on Manipura Chakra, one gets the knowledge of the construction of the body, the seven Dhatus etc. By practising concentration on (the Chakra at) the pit of the throat (Visuddha Chakra), comes the removal of hunger and thirst. By practising concentration on Anahata Chakra (at the heart) comes the knowledge of the mind. By the practice of concentration on Sahasrara Chakra (on the head) comes the Darsana of Siddhas. These are some of the important internal Chakras for the practice of concentration.

You can concentrate on some of the abstract ideas such as purity, courage, love, mercy, etc. You can feel 'I am purity,' 'I am full of mercy,' 'I am full of love,' 'I am full of courage' etc. You can even concentrate on ideas such as, 'God is full of Love,' 'God is Omnipresent,' 'God is full of Light,' 'God is full of Knowledge.'

In concentration you will have only one Vritti or wave in the mind-lake. The mind assumes the form of only one object. All other operations of the mind are suspended.

MEDITA

'*Dhyanam Nirvishayam Manah*'—That state of the mind wherein there are no Vishaya or sensual thoughts is meditation.

A continuous flow of perception or thought is Dhyana or meditation. There is continuous current in the mind on one object like the flow of water in a river.

Meditation is the keeping of an unceasing flow of God-consciousness. It is the flow of continuous thought of one thing or God or Atman. Meditation follows concentration. Meditation is regular flow of thought with regard to the object of concentration.

Meditation is the only way for attaining immortality and eternal bliss.

Meditation is of two kinds viz., Saguna (concrete) meditation and Nirguna (abstract) meditation. In concrete meditation, the student concentrates on the form of Lord Krishna, Rama, Siva, Hari, Gayatri or Sri Devi. In abstract meditation, he concentrates the whole energy of the mind on one idea of God or Atman and avoids comparisons of memories and all other ideas. The one idea fills the whole mind.

Saguna meditation is meditation on a Murti or form of the Lord. This is concrete form of meditation for people of devotional temperament. This is meditation with Gunas or attributes of God. Repeat the Name of the Lord. Think of His attributes, Omniscience, Omnipotence, Omnipresence etc. The mind will be filled with purity. Enthrone the Lord in the lotus of your heart amidst a blazing light. Mentally think of His feet, legs, chest, head, hands and the ornaments and dress and again and again come to His face. Again and again repeat this process.

Saguna meditation is meditation on a form. Select any Murti you like best, either Siva, Vishnu, Rama or Krishna, according to your inclination or taste. An archer first aims at grosser objects. Then he takes up medium objects. Finally he shoots at finer and subtle objects. Even so one should take to Saguna meditation to start with and when the mind is trained and disciplined well, he can have Nirakara, Nirguna meditation. Saguna meditation removes Vikshepa.

Meditate on the mental picture of the Murti or Form half to two hours only in the Trikuti (the space between the two eye-brows) or in the heart. See and feel that the Ishta is present in every object in the universe. When you meditate, mentally repeat the Mantra of the Ishta. Feel that Sattvic qualities from the Ishta flows towards you. Feel that you possess this Sattvic Bhavana. You will have Darsana of your Ishta, if you are sincere in your practice.

To start with, meditate for half an hour in the morning from 4 to 4-30 and for half an hour in the evening from 6 to 6-30 and gradually you can increase the time upto 3 hours for each sitting. Morning time is the best for meditation. The mind is refreshed after sound sleep. Further Sattva predominates in the system as in the surrounding atmosphere.

Nirguna meditation is Aham-graha-Upasana. This is meditation on Om. This is meditation on an abstract idea. Sit in Padmasana. Repeat Om mentally. Keep the meaning of Om always in the mind. Feel that you are the all-pervading. You are Infinite Light. Feel that you are the Suddha-Sat-Chit-Ananda Vyapaka Atman, Nitya Suddha Buddha Mukta, eternally free Brahman. Feel that you are Chaitanya. Feel that you are the Akhanda, Paripurna, Ekarasa, Shanta, Infinite, Eternal, Unchanging Existence. Lip repetition will not do. It should be through heart, head and soul. Your whole soul should feel that you are the subtle, all-pervading intelligence. This feeling should be kept up continuously.

Negate the body idea when you repeat Om mentally. When you chant Om feel: Infinity I am. All Light I am. All Joy I am. All Glory I am. All Power I am. All Knowledge I am. All Ananda I am.

Meditate on the above ideas constantly. Constant effort with zeal and enthusiasm is indispensable. Repeat mentally the above ideas incessantly. You will realise. You will have Atma-Darsana.

Meditate constantly and intensely: I am that Brahman or the Intelligence Absolute, Bliss Absolute, Existence Absolute, ever free, Immortal, eternal, self-effulgent, self-luminous, self-contained, birthless, decayless, deathless, changeless, timeless, spaceless, limitless, secondless.

Even in Nirguna meditation (formless) there will be an abstract mental image in the beginning of Sadhana. The abstract image will vanish eventually. When you meditate, negate the names and forms. Do not mistake either the physical body or the mind, the Prana, the intellect or the Indriyas for the pure eternal Atman. The highest Self is entirely distinct from these. Meditate on the above ideas and bring the Bhava during work also. You can take up any of the following formulae: "I am the All. I am in all. I am the Immortal Self in all. I am living Truth." Bring back the mind to the point again and again if the mind wanders. You can rotate the mind from one formula to another if the mind wanders and finally fix it on one formula only, when the mind has become steady. The mind will become now like the steady flame of a lamp in a windless place. You will rest in your own Svarupa, thoughtless state of pure bliss. Samadhi or superconscious state will ensue now.

SAMADHI

The meditation is Samadhi when it shines with the object of meditation alone, as it were devoid of itself. The thinker and the meditated become one. The mind becomes the Dhyeyarupa. the separate notions 'contemplation,' 'contemplated' and 'contemplator' vanish. In the state of Samadhi the aspirant is not conscious of any external or internal objects. Just as the arrow-maker, having his mind engrossed in the arrow, knew not the king passing by his side, so also, the Yogi knows not any thing when he is deep in his meditation.

Samadhi or blissful divine experience arises when the ego and the mind are dissolved. It is a state to be attained by one's own effort. It is limitless, divisionless and infinite. When this experience is realised, the mind, desires, actions and feelings of joy and sorrow vanish into a void.

Samadhi is of various kinds. But of all of them there are only very few important ones.

The Samadhi experienced by a Bhakta is Bhava Samadhi. The devotee attains the state through Bhava and Mahabhava. A Bhakta who meditates on the form of

Lord Krishna will see Krishna and Krishna only everywhere, when he is established in Samadhi. All other forms will disappear. This is one kind of Samadhi. He will see himself as Krishna. Gopis of Brindavan, Gouranga and Ekanath had this experience. Those who meditate on the all-pervading Krishna will have another kind of cosmic experience, the consciousness of whole Virat.

Again there are two other varieties of Samadhi, viz., Savikalpa and Nirvikalpa Samadhi. In the first variety there is Triputi or the triad, viz., knower, knowledge and knowable, or seer, sight and seen. The Samskaras are not destroyed. In the latter, the Samskaras are totally fried or destroyed. There is no Triputi in Nirvikalpa Samadhi.

Samprajnata is another name for Savikalpa Samadhi. Asamprajnata is another name for Nirvikalpa Samadhi.

In Nirvikalpa Samadhi there is no ego-consciousness. Ego and mind melt and fuse in Brahman. The pure mind assumes the form of Brahman. This is known as Nirbija Samadhi. There is no prop for the mind in this Samadhi. The Samskaras are fried in toto. Savikalpa Samadhi deepens into Nirvikalpa Samadhi. There is no idea of any kind in Nirvikalpa Samadhi. It is thoughtless Absolute Consciousness.

Nirvikalpa means that in which there is no Vikalpa. That which is not associated with any idea is Nirvikalpa. No imagination, no functioning of mind or intellect. All Vrittis totally cease. There is only pure Consciousness or Awareness. All the Samskaras and Vasanas are fried in toto. All names and forms are burnt up. Asti-Bhati-Priya only remains. Asti-Bhati-Priya is Sat-Chit-Ananda. That which ever exists is Asti; that which shines is Bhati. This is

Absolute Consciousness. And that which gives happiness is Priya; this is unalloyed Bliss, Ananda. In Nirvikalpa Samadhi the mind is freed from distraction, attachments. it rests unmoved like the flame of a lamp sheltered from the wind.

In Samadhi or Superconsciousness the student gets himself merged in the Lord. The senses, the mind and the intellect cease functioning. Just as river joins the ocean, the individual soul mixes with the Supreme Soul. The Samadhi bestows Supreme Knowledge, and one is freed from the wheel of births and deaths and gets Kaivalya (Moksha) or liberation.